Parenting-Wise

Quick Tips for
Raising Them Right

Parenting-Wise

Quick Tips for Raising Them Right

LAURIE LAFORTUNE

WINDWORD GROUP
PUBLISHING & MEDIA

Copyright © 2019 Laurie Lafortune
All rights reserved.
ISBN:-10:1-947527-01-0
ISBN-13: 978-1-947527-01-0

Some of this material has been written and distributed previously online.

DEDICATION

This book is dedicated to my family.

CONTENTS

1. What's your parenting style? — 1
2. New baby, new worries — 5
3. Adjusting to your new role — 8
4. Your child's brain — 11
5. How parents can help with healthy brain development — 13
6. Is my child alright? — 16
7. Fathers and mothers: different parenting styles — 19
8. Having a conversation with a baby: The beginning of language development — 21
9. How parents can help build literacy skills. — 25
10. Choosing quality child care — 29
11. Parents need to look after themselves — 35
12. Spending time in nature — 37
13. Playtime for preschoolers — 39
14. Getting the kids to play outside — 42
15. Young children and quiet times — 46
16. What does school success mean to you? — 49
17. Be involved with your child's school — 51
18. What a high school teacher would like parents to know — 54
19. Connecting with kids — 57
20. Positive conversations with teens — 60
21. Spanking — 63
22. Avoid negative behavior before it starts: remember HALT — 67
23. Dealing with the worst time of day for family stress — 69
24. Helping your child to be respectful — 72
25. Understanding your child's temperament — 75
26. Should parents make their kids say, "I'm sorry"? — 78
27. What's wrong with praise? — 81

28. Why do toddlers have such challenging behaviors? 84
29. Temper tantrums 87
30. Encouraging independence 91
31. Should kids do chores? 94
32. Kids and phones 97
33. Kids and allowances 100
34. Shopping and financial literacy 103
35. Helping your teens to be realistic about money 106
36. Should your teen have a part-time or summer job? 109
37. Helping young children when natural disasters strike 112
38. Last thoughts 115

PREFACE

Sharing in your children's lives as you watch their growth and development is one of the greatest experiences anyone can have. But for me and for most parents, it was surprising (and shocking) how much our lives changed with the arrival of a baby. *Everything* changes! Trying to manage the new situation is hard work and kind of scary, as you worry if you are doing the right things for your children. Each day can bring new challenges and new questions.

Through the years of raising my three children, and now helping to care for grandchildren, I've learned a lot and was encouraged to write this book to share some of my experiences and suggestions with other parents. With brief chapters that can be read quickly and in any order, I offer some strategies and ideas to help with the tough and complex role of being a parent. I hope you'll find some common-sense tips and some fun suggestions. My ideas come from lifelong learning and employment in the human services field, and from my experiences as a parent, teacher, and early childhood educator. This book is not intended to be a comprehensive parenting manual.

Please remember that no parent is perfect. We all do our best, but in the thousands of interactions we have with our children over the years, we will sometimes make mistakes, and wish we could take back impatient words or certain hasty decisions. But overall, our love, guidance and wisdom can create a foundation for positive, successful parenting. And the wonder of a child's development into a unique individual will make up for all the work, worry and sleepless nights.

I am not a medical professional. The opinions and information in these topics are not intended nor implied to be a substitute for professional medical advice. Always seek the advice of a physician or other qualified health care provider for any questions you may have regarding a health condition or with concerns about your child's development.

Please note also that I have used the pronouns 'he' and 'she' interchangeably throughout the book.

1
WHAT'S YOUR PARENTING STYLE?

As a parent, you are your child's first teacher and you have a great influence on him or her. Whether you intend it or not, your parenting style will have an impact on your child. If your goal is to have a child who can think for himself, make good judgements and regulate his own behavior, then you need to use a parenting style that will encourage and support that goal. This might be similar to how you were raised, or it might be quite different.

According to parenting education programs, there are three basic styles of parenting. For successful parenting, you need to think about what parenting style you were raised with, what style you currently use and whether that is the type of parent you want to be. An authoritarian parent is a parent whose actions and words come from a place of total authority. You can also think of the authoritarian parent as a dictator, or the boss of the whole household. The child has absolutely no say at all and would not get to express an opinion. The parent would regularly say things like, "Because I said so." or "There will be no discussion."

The parent treats each of her children the same, regardless of their temperament, needs, age and the situation. This style of parenting has obedience as the primary goal. But if you hope that your children grow up to be adults who can think for themselves, solve problems, have confidence, show courage, and make their own decisions, then be aware that dictator-style, authoritarian parenting isn't going to achieve that. If your goal is to have a child who always obeys, this method might work while a child is young, but your child will almost certainly rebel as a preteen or teen, sometimes in dangerous ways.

The other end of the spectrum on parenting is the permissive parent or 'doormat'. This is the parent who is not at all the leader in the family. The child has as much say as the parent. The permissive parent might say things like, "Well, if you want it that much, you can have it,". "I'll do that homework for you," or "You can have it if you'll just stop crying." And if the permissive parent doesn't actually say those things, her actions send the same message. Giving in and buying things to keep the peace, giving candy or other treats to stop a child in a tantrum, putting herself and others last after anything the child might want—all these actions send a message that the parent is a doormat.

A permissive parent tries to make sure her child is never disappointed, unhappy, frustrated, angry or sad. That's an impossible task, and even if it were possible, you are not doing your child any favors. In the future, how will this child be able to cope with obstacles or difficulties when the parent is not around to satisfy every wish or to make everything okay?

The third and middle-ground type of parent is the authoritative parent; not authoritarian or permissive, but *authoritative*. This parent supports and helps his children, listens to their opinions, is fair and kind, but does not forget who is the parent and who is the child. This style of parenting reflects the belief that children need a parent, not another friend. This parent knows that a child needs an adult whom they can count on to provide for their needs with fair but not harsh discipline, based on the real world. This parent would say things like:

> "Let's all take a turn talking about what we want to do today, and then we will make a decision that works best."
>
> "I know you don't want to stop watching your show, but we have to turn it off now and go have supper."
>
> "Even if some of your friends are allowed, it's not something that I think is safe. I know you are disappointed, but the answer is no."

So, when the authoritative parent says "no," there is a reason, (told to the child), and the parent listens to the child's point of view. But in the end, the final decision belongs to the adult who is responsible for the well-being of everyone in the family. It's not always easy to resist a child's opinion especially in the teenage years, but children do need a parent, not another buddy. Kids have lots of friends, but you are their only parent.

Think about whether your parenting goals align with the type of parenting you are doing. Are there parenting skills you could improve upon? Ask yourself for example, whether several families don't want your child to visit or play at their home? Do other kids tell your child he's bossy or mean and they don't want to play with him? Does your child's childcare provider, teacher or coach have difficulty getting your child to cooperate? If so, you might be acting as a permissive parent, and even if this is fine with you in your own home, it might not be accepted away from your home. Your caring and desire to protect your child from all disappointments and frustrations have gone too far and will create negative consequences for your child. Your child has not had the chance to learn to follow adult direction, or to get along with others.

On the other hand, is your child very withdrawn, quiet or fearful in a group of kids, or at daycare or school?

Is he afraid to ask for anything? Does she have difficulty making decisions or problem-solving? Maybe you've been overly authoritarian and too strict. Your wish to have a well-behaved child and to set clear limits may have been taken too far. If you want your child to be independent and eventually able to make choices and solve problems on his own, then you have to teach those skills and allow him to make some choices now.

So, make it your goal to be an authoritative parent. Use your parenting skills to take charge, but also to allow freedom within limits. This successful parenting style will encourage mutual respect and communication, while helping your child to be a happy, accepted child, teen and adult.

2
NEW BABY, NEW WORRIES

One thing that parents never expect is how much they will worry while looking after their baby. So many things can go wrong and there seem to be so many pitfalls. It's the uncertainty—you just never know what each day will bring. Because the baby is growing and changing so quickly, just when you think you have it all figured out, something changes.

The baby is breathing noisily through his nose OR the baby is breathing so softly that you keep checking to make sure he's still alive.

He's crying a lot OR he's not crying much.

She wants to be held all the time OR she cries even when you cuddle her.

He's pooping all the time OR he hasn't pooped for two days.

She's falling asleep before she finishes feeding OR she seems to sleep hardly at all!

She's always hungry OR it seems like she's not getting enough.

So, what's a new parent supposed to do? What's the right thing?

Most parents say they get advice from their doctor about the baby's growth and development, but we don't see doctors that often. So, parents go online. But going online for answers can sometimes make you worry even more! There are so many opinions and so many potential problems, illnesses and conditions that people describe that it can give you even more things to worry about.

If you do get your health and development advice online, be sure you are at a reputable, credible website. Try the health region websites or the government health websites. Avoid sponsored sites—they might try to create a new worry or need in you just to get you to buy their product. Remember, anyone can post anything! There is just so much information! Lots of the stories you read have incorrect advice that is not approved by medical experts. Some of the ideas and suggestions posted are unsafe for babies. *Always* consider the source of the "information".

If you prefer written material and books about baby care, your health region will have pamphlets and recommended reading. Ask if there is something that contains "when to call the doctor," things to be concerned about, what's normal and what's not, or something along those lines. That is really why and when most new parents worry. Books on baby care and development that are authored by medical doctors and approved by pediatric associations are the ones to look for.

Most communities have a health line that you can call or text to ask questions about anything related to health. Health care professionals answer these, and no question is considered unimportant. Other help is available from public health nurses, home visitors and midwives who will come to your home to pay a visit. You can ask them about all your concerns and questions. Call your local social services or community services to see if there is a support service like this available for you as a new parent.

Although some baby care advice has changed over time, grandparents can be a real help. Hopefully, they won't want to interfere with how you are doing things. They might not offer information, but if you ask their opinion, they'll be glad to talk. You might as well take advantage of their wisdom and hear about their mistakes.

But one of the most helpful things for a new parent is to have friends who are young parents, too. This gives you a support network of experienced parents to talk things over with. I remember learning how to swaddle like a pro from a friend who had three children before I had my first. The relief that gave to my overstimulated crying baby was so soothing, both to him and me. I also learned from a friend to let my toddler chew on cold celery or a cold wet washcloth for teething pain.

So, try not to worry too much. Don't be afraid to ask questions! No one expects you to be an expert in this new, overwhelming role. You (and your baby) will be just fine!

3
ADJUSTING TO YOUR NEW ROLE

Here is some information that might be helpful for new parents who are feeling overwhelmed with all the new tasks and responsibilities and who need some parenting help. As part of parent self-care for new parents, it's helpful to keep a sense of humor, to realize that no new parent really knows exactly what they are doing, and that all parents worry about doing the right thing.

None of the resources or parenting books for moms and dads fully prepare you for the reality of being a new parent. You learn a lot of things on your own, fast. And there often isn't time to search for parenting resources. It's a brand-new job, probably the most important one you'll ever do, and there is no manager, HR department or trainer to help you in this new role. You'll be taken by surprise by a lot of new baby events...

For example, just because he breast fed for over an hour, doesn't mean he won't want more 10 or 20 minutes later.

A package of diapers will last five days less than you expected.

Same with a package of baby wipes.

Newborn clothes only fit for less than a week, if you even use them at all!

Never assume that because you changed a dirty diaper, there won't be more coming out very soon.

Don't stand in the line of fire when changing a baby boy's diaper; keep a cloth over top. Even newborns can pee record-breaking distances.

Babies cry a lot!

Babies don't sleep for very long at a time.

Taking a two-minute shower feels as good as a full spa visit.

A baby who doesn't walk or crawl can somehow create a load of laundry every day, and that's not counting diapers!

How can it be afternoon already and you haven't had time to get dressed?

Having a baby is the biggest change you will ever experience. It's incredible how much your lifestyle, routines, tasks, personal time and relationships will change. It's the kind of thing that no one really understands until they've experienced for themselves. But even with all the challenges and surprises, you'll be amazed at what you can manage. Your parenting skills will get better and before you know it, you'll have mastered this brand-new role of looking after an infant.

Just when you are getting comfortable in your parenting skills and you think maybe you've got this new job figured out, things will change. Because of the fast rate of child development in the first year, new challenges will come up almost daily. Your baby's daily routine will change, he'll be awake more, and start to smile, laugh, coo and babble. He may have days when it seems he is eating constantly, as he rapidly grows and develops. He'll start creeping, crawling and eventually walking, creating a whole new set of challenges to keep him safe for you as a parent.

Have confidence in your abilities, ask for help and advice when you need it, and enjoy the amazing experience of being a parent—the most challenging and important job you will ever do.

4
YOUR CHILD'S BRAIN

Parents think a lot about the weight and height of their children, carefully recording the stats on a chart or in a baby book. But what about a baby's brain? What actually is going on in the brain as a baby grows? Here's a basic overview of brain development in the early years.

The brain begins to develop early in pregnancy, just shortly after conception. Brain cells, or neurons, are formed and at birth a baby will have almost all the neurons he or she will ever have. But that doesn't mean that the brain is finished developing. It is from birth to age five that more brain development will happen than in any other time of life. But if it's not new brain cells that are being created, then what is going on in the brain?

At birth, a baby's brain is about one quarter of adult size. By age one, the brain has doubled in size. By age three, the brain is 80 per cent of adult size and by age five, it's 90 per cent. Most of this growth is due to the development of the synapses between the brain cells (neurons). The synapses are connections between the neurons, and it is these connections that allow the neurons to communicate with each other and organize into circuits or networks. These connections happen very quickly in the early years of life. About 700 synapses or connections per second are formed—an incredible rate of growth!

Another important process taking place in the brain is myelination. Myelin is a fatty material that coats the axon of the brain cell, acting as a protection for the cell. Similar to insulation, myelination improves how quickly and efficiently messages are transmitted in the brain. In very young children, messages move more slowly in the brain, since myelination is not yet complete. This explains why a two-year-old might have a long pause before responding to you; it simply is taking longer for his brain to process the message it is receiving.

But what about genes? Genes are important and do provide the blueprint for the brain, but it is the environment and early experiences that influence the brain's growth and development. The genes are like a seed, and the experiences and home environment are the soil, sunlight, weeding and care that affect how well that seed will grow. Brain synapses, networks and circuits are created by the experiences that a baby has. A baby's brain develops through his senses. Every touch, smell, taste, feeling and sound creates connections in the brain. That is why it is so crucial that a developing child has many varied positive experiences. This rapid growth in synapses means that a two-year-old actually has more synapses than an adult. What happens is that unused synapses are 'pruned back' and synapses and networks that are used more frequently become stronger and remain as part of the brain. Neuroscientists believe that the pruning process makes the brain more efficient. The brain continues to adapt, develop and change throughout life, with another major growth period during adolescence. Complex cognitive functions are among the last to develop.

Remember, more brain development happens during the first few years of life than in any later years.

5
HOW PARENTS CAN HELP WITH HEALTHY BRAIN DEVELOPMENT

A key point about building a healthy brain is that a child's brain is impacted by all experiences, through their senses of touch, taste, hearing, feelings, smell and sight. The brain physically changes based on these experiences and the environment that a child grows up in. So, it's very important for parents to know how they can support healthy brain development. The brain is far more impressionable and adaptable in the first five years than in any other time of life. Just look at how much easier it is for a child to learn a new language, or to skate, ski or swim than it is to learn these new skills as an adult. Or think about how much change and learning happens from a newborn to an 18-month-old. The toddler can walk, talk, sing, solve simple problems, and definitely shows personality—quite a change from the newborn state and a clear indication of the scope of brain development that has happened. Learning all these new skills depends on the development of connections and networks in the brain. This adaptability, (or "plasticity" as neuroscientists call it) has both a positive and negative side. It means that young children's brains are more open to learning and new experiences so that new skills are learned more easily. But, it also means that young children's brains can be easily harmed if babies or young children are in an uncaring or stressful environment, or if they are neglected or abused.

So here are some ways to help a baby's brain to develop. The most basic and earliest way to build a healthy brain is to have a healthy pregnancy. Good nutrition, adequate exercise and sleep, having no alcohol, or other harmful substances, and regular prenatal care from a health professional will help ensure that a healthy foundation for brain development is made.

As soon as a baby is born, she can see, hear, taste, smell and respond to touch. Give your baby bright, colorful objects to look at. Show her the light coming in a window, shadows and most importantly, the human faces of you and your family. For newborns, the distance should be 12-18 inches. Babies also like simple black and white designs. Use mobiles and hanging decorations and change them often. Go out for walks and let your baby see the world around her. Show your baby herself in a (safety) mirror.

Play soft, gentle music. Some babies are upset by loud music, so you may want to save the country and rock songs for when she's older. Talk to your baby a lot. Describe or narrate what you are doing and what you see. Read to her, sing to her, recite verses and nursery rhymes. The more words and sounds your baby hears, the more the brain will develop. Television and recorded talking will not create the same brain connections as your own voice and eye contact do.

Respond to a baby's needs quickly and consistently. By taking care of a baby's needs when she cries, you are teaching her to trust you, that you (and other caregivers) are there to care for her and will try to figure out what she needs. She will learn to trust you. Remember that crying is a baby's way to communicate. Never ignore a crying infant.

Give your baby lots of attention. Keep her near you. Talk with her, make eye contact frequently and have other family members pay attention to the baby as well. Smile often when talking with the baby. Your baby will like to be touched and carried and will enjoy the rhythm of an adult's movement. She may also enjoy being held in an upright position and being held while you dance or move from side to side. Most babies enjoy walks in a stroller or rides in a car.

Play is critical for brain development. The brain doesn't develop by passive watching of a screen or from direct instructions from an adult. A baby learns by being actively involved in play experiences. Babies learn by doing. So, baby-proof your home and then give your baby time and space to explore.

A healthy body supports a healthy brain, so be sure to continue regular visits with your health professional. Have hearing, vision, and routine developmental milestone checks as your baby grows. Provide a nutritious, balanced diet, and don't forget that adequate sleep is important for healthy brain development.

Remember, it's the positive experiences and interactions that help a brain to grow. Babies and young children thrive when adults are warm, loving, and consistently respond to them.

6
IS MY CHILD ALRIGHT?

The first time your child plays with other kids, or goes to daycare, preschool or kindergarten you will notice other children's skills and abilities and you start thinking about how your own child compares. You may notice that some children talk like little adults, while others use very few words. Some children can talk clearly, while other kids' words are very hard to understand. Some children will be printing letters, drawing and coloring detailed pictures, while others are holding a pencil in a fist-like grip and do not attempt to draw or print. Some children climb easily on the playground equipment and can throw and kick a ball well. Others seem less coordinated in their movements. Some will be able to put on their own jackets and boots, while others struggle. You wonder if your child is developing as she should, or if there is a problem or delay. Or are some of the other kids advanced for their age? What are the areas of development a parent should be aware of and what are typical abilities for a child of a certain age?

The areas of development include cognitive or intellectual development, social skills, physical, (which includes fine and large motor skills), emotional development and language or communication skills. A child who is developing appropriately for his age in these five areas is more likely to be able to meet the challenges of group settings such as preschool, daycare and kindergarten. Many studies have shown that children who do well in kindergarten continue to succeed in the early grades and are more likely to complete high school.

But how does a parent know what is typical? There is such a range of abilities in children. You wonder—is my kid doing okay?

Parent educators and health care professionals recommend that parents be aware of *developmental milestones*, which are a set of skills or tasks that most children do within a certain age range. Parents who know the developmental milestones will be able to tell if their child is developing within the typical age range for various tasks. For example, you would expect an infant to smile at two months of age. Walking develops anywhere between nine and 15 months. By 12 months, a baby can say at least one word, and by 18 months, a toddler usually can say 15 words. But parents should avoid comparing their child with others or with older siblings, because every child is an individual and develops at their own pace. If your child is not doing things that are expected by the older age limit for the developmental milestone, or if he had the ability but then lost it, you should talk to your health professional about your concerns. One of my sons walked at 11 months, and another didn't walk without assistance until 15 months. I did ask my doctor about this, since it was much later than I had expected. I was reassured by my doctor that my child was still within the age range for this milestone. When my son finally let go of the furniture, he was sturdy and balanced. He fell very rarely and progressed quickly to running and climbing, much faster than my other children. I learned later that a cautious temperament, as this child has, is often related to later walking. It's as if the child is thinking, "I won't try it until I am sure I can do it well."

If your child does have a delay, it's always best to work on the area of development as soon as possible. The earlier the intervention, the better.

Regularly provide opportunities for your child for active physical play, interaction with other children and adults, reading and conversation, and play materials that encourage exploration and problem-solving. Parenting resources are available from health clinics, your doctor and online that outline typical development with suggestions for activities parents can provide to encourage various skills.

7
FATHERS AND MOTHERS: DIFFERENT PARENTING STYLES

Nowadays, most fathers are very involved as parents, compared to fathers in the 1970s or 80s. Despite their involvement, sometimes fathers still feel left out, slotted into the traditional role of breadwinner or as secondary in raising their children. Pictures of moms and kids, programs called 'Moms Morning Out, Mom and Tot playtime, and so many other messages come at us showing fathers as not being as involved as mothers. Or worse, Dad is often shown as being a bit of a well-meaning goof.

But fathers are very important to their kids. Their involvement supports the emotional development of their children. They provide a different kind of play and offer different learning experiences. Often, it's Dad who loves to answer the never ending 'Why?' questions, who shows kids all the new technology or sports equipment, who loves to build and fix things, who provides the outdoor experiences, and who introduces the kids to sports.

Over forty years of research have proven that the more actively involved a dad is in his children's lives, the better off the children will be. And this is true right from birth. Babies are more likely to be confident in new situations, feel secure and eager to explore, and be more sociable if they have involved fathers. Children with involved fathers do better academically. Studies have shown that Dads use more what, where and why questions when talking with their toddlers, which helps with speech and language development. These findings are true for boys and girls.

Spending time with your kids is essential for them and including your kids in your interests will create a very special lifelong relationship. And if anyone thinks that Dads are more important to their boys, study after study has shown that both boys and girls benefit from time with Dads.

Fathers of young children are doing more with their young children than in previous generations. And many community programs and organizations are providing opportunities for Dads to participate in programs and events specifically for them. "Daddy and Me" playtimes offer the opportunity for new fathers to meet other Dads and to enjoy time with their kids. It's always helpful to spend time with other parents, especially other Dads, who have in common the wish to do their very best job as a parent. Media portrayals of dads are changing, and more are recognizing the important role that dads have.

It's not which parent is better, or more important, but rather recognizing that the two adults are complementary for a child's well-being and development.

8
HAVING A CONVERSATION WITH A BABY

How can you have a conversation with a baby when she can't talk yet? It's actually pretty easy and natural once you get the hang of it. AND it's important for a baby's cognitive, social and emotional development. A recent study in *Pediatrics* showed a large increase in the number of children with communication disorders over the past ten years. So, parents should try to do all they can to encourage speech and language development in the context of loving interactions.

Parenting books recommend one-on-one conversation as most effective in the development of communication skills. This back and forth, with the parent repeating and responding to a baby's sounds, and the baby responding again, is sometimes called 'serve and return', using the analogy of a tennis game. This can be a powerful way to explain the best way for parents to respond and initiate conversations with their babies and young children. The 'serve and return' interaction can be started by the baby or the caregiver. Every time a baby makes a vocalization (the serve) the caregiver would respond, by imitating the sound or by expanding on the sound into words or a few sentences (the return). The caregiver should talk, sing or coo, making sounds towards the baby (the serve), and the baby will respond with her own sounds, or simply with eye contact and paying attention (the return). Eye contact is very important with babies. Even before the baby makes any sounds, she will be responding very subtly to your voice with eye contact.

Parents need to be aware that it's never too early to start having conversations with a baby. The foundation for speech is created long before a baby starts to talk. In utero, babies hear the sounds of the world. Research shows that newborn babies just one day old can identify their mother's voice.

Conversations with a baby make brain connections that contribute to speech development. It's helpful to be aware of typical milestones in speech and language development. At about eight weeks, babies will start cooing, making vowel sounds like ah, ah. At around three to four months, babies start babbling (sounds such as ma ma ma ma, buhbuhbuh). At six to eight months, babies will babble back, in response to a parent's vocalizations and words. This is when some of the babble can be recognized as sounding like simple words, and parents can repeat back the words they think they have heard. So if a baby says "ba, ba", the parent should repeat it and then expand on the syllable, saying, "ball, ball. Do you want your ball?" The excitement of hearing a baby make sounds that resemble real words encourages parents to smile, repeat and continue the verbal interaction, encouraging the baby to vocalize even more. Between seven and 12 months, a baby makes purposeful gestures and motions (like waving bye-bye, or pointing to something), and at this point she is using non-verbal language. She can bring you an item that when asked and enjoys repetitive songs and verses. She'll turn and look when called by name. At around 12 months, she will usually say her first word. This is different from babbling, because she now understands that the word symbolizes the object. So when she says "baa" and picks up a ball, or "Da-da", when her dad arrives, she has started the exciting process of talking. Other common first words are "Hi" and "No."

One of the easiest ways to provide lots of words and one-on-one interactions is for a parent to narrate the day. Describe what is happening, making lots of eye contact and responding to any vocalizing the baby does. "Baby talk" has been shown to be a helpful, effective way to encourage communication skills. So, a conversation with a young infant and her parent might sound like this:

Parent: "I see you are yawning. Are you getting tired? A nice warm bath will be fun. Oh look, you made me yawn too! Now let's see how your diaper is..."

Baby: "Babababba."

Parent: "Oh, are you telling me a story? Are you telling me you want a bath, bath bath? It's fun kicking your legs, isn't it? Kick, kick, kick. Let's get the water ready"... and so on.

This running narrative might make you feel awkward (or like you are doing a play-by-play commentary) but just think of every word and interaction as a building block for language development and give it a try. If this narration comes naturally to a parent, that's great! Because it's absolutely the best way to encourage speech and language development. If you feel a bit odd or strange talking to a small infant, think about your pet. Lots of adults have no problem talking to their dog or cat, saying things like, "I've got your leash, you know that means we are going for a walk." Or "It looks like you need some food," or "You like having your ears rubbed, don't you?" If you can talk to your pet, you can talk to your baby!

Remember that your baby will understand many words (receptive language), long before she starts to speak. (expressive language). Her vocabulary will grow as she hears your words. She will imitate the sounds she hears, and then suddenly words will emerge with new ones being tried out almost daily. Only about half of these sounds may be recognizable as words. Clear pronunciation develops with time.

Speech and language are the foundation for reading and writing. Language development at the age of two years predicts children's performance on entry at school. So, having a conversation, reading, talking and singing, with lots of eye contact and cuddling, will give a baby a great start!

9
HOW PARENTS CAN HELP BUILD LITERACY SKILLS

Studies have shown that children who are behind in reading in school in the third grade often continue to fall behind and are four times less likely to graduate high school than other children. The first three grades of school are very important in learning to read, but the foundation for reading is laid at home, long before formal schooling begins. Parents can play a key role in helping their children be successful in school before school begins, not by teaching them to read, but by supporting the development of literacy. Parents should start as early and as frequently as possible with simple communication activities.

First of all, as with every action your child observes, set a good example; show your child that reading and writing are fun and important to you and other adults. Have books and magazines around the house, accessible to children. Let your child see you doing literacy activities. Such things as making a grocery list, sending emails or texts, writing notes or cards, reading books or tablets—all these activities send a message about the importance of reading and writing.

Literacy Activities with Babies

Read and tell stories to your baby from birth (or sooner!) Your baby will listen to your voice and will hear words, rhythm and expression, making the connection between words and meaning. When your baby coos and babbles, he is trying to talk to you. Encourage and respond to these sounds. Talk throughout the day, telling your baby what you are doing, and what is happening next," I'm making your lunch and then we'll eat." Or "I'll wash your face and then we'll get dressed to go for a walk." Narrate and describe activities throughout the day, to increase the number of words that your baby hears. The number of words a baby hears is strongly linked to later reading ability. In the car, in a line-up, or waiting for appointments—these are all opportunities to provide literacy activities. Sing favorite songs, recite verses and nursery rhymes, and bring along favorite books in your bag.

Books for babies should be durable and easy to clean. A baby's fine motor coordination is just developing; it is difficult for them to turn paper pages and easy to tear them. Do not worry about teaching a baby to be careful when handling books; simply provide books that can stand up to a baby's use. Thick cardboard pages, plasticized or cloth books with few pages are good choices. Babies will put corners of books in their mouths and chew on them. After exploring a book in that way, the baby will open the book. Later on, a baby will bring a book for you to read aloud. Point to pictures in books and identify what they are. At this stage, there's no need to read the exact words of a story, just make up a story based on the pictures.

Literacy Activities for Toddlers and Preschoolers

Continue providing books that are durable. Join the library and get your child their own library card. Allow your child to choose books at the library and buy books as gifts or special treats. Some parents avoid the "I wants" when shopping by allowing their child to buy a book, rather than toys or junk food. Have a low, accessible shelf or area for your child's book collection. Read out loud daily (aim for 20 minutes a day) to your child and have books in his or her room as well as around the house. Let your child choose books for you to read aloud. Children typically have favorites and may ask for the same book over and over, enjoying the predictability and repetition. You may find that, well before learning to read, your child can memorize a favorite book exactly and will repeat the words perfectly, knowing exactly when to turn the page. Ask questions like, "What happens next?" with familiar books, and "What's that?" while pointing to pictures. Alphabet books and counting books are great for preschoolers and they enjoy reciting letters and numbers. Around age four or five, children can often recognize the first letter of their name (or many letters) and it's fun for them to find letters in a book.

As children get older, they can handle longer books with paper pages. Have books in many places around the house, including the child's bedroom. Your child can then look quietly at a book during nap or quiet times or before sleep. Continue to read together daily. If your child has an interest in a topic, find books on that subject to enjoy together. Talk about the books you are reading, using open-ended questions about the plot and characters, such as, "Why do you think he did that?" "Would you like to do that?" "What do you think is going to happen next?" "What was your favorite part of the story?" Ask your child to tell the story in their own words, and encourage them to explore books with younger siblings, 'reading' a story themselves.

Successful parenting includes giving your child a good start to learning, and reading is a key component. Children learn best from a caring adult, so enjoy these special times with your children.

10
CHOOSING QUALITY CHILD CARE

For most parents, child care is a requirement. A child will spend many hours in a child care setting while parents are at work, and the environment is important for a child's safety and development. There is a huge difference between simple babysitting and an early learning and care arrangement. When it's time to go back to your job, one of the biggest challenges is to find high quality child care. What should parents look for when making a choice?

There are two basic types of child care: family home care and center-based care. Family home child care takes place in a caregiver's own home. The caregiver typically has young children of her own and offers child care to other children in her own home. The group of children is small, multi-age, and the home would be a place that is somewhat like what an infant or preschooler is used to, with a kitchen, play area, bedrooms and usually an outdoor yard. The caregiver is not typically required to have formal training in early childhood education. There is usually only the one adult in the home, providing care. Some family child care homes are approved or licensed by the government or by an agency contracted by the government. Most are not, since anyone can start up a private child care business in their own home. Private operators who are not affiliated with or approved by an agency must still abide by the rule for the maximum number of children allowed. This varies from region to region. These numbers can be larger if more than one caregiver is present in the home. Numbers include the caregivers' own children, and also set out maximum numbers of children by age, reflecting the greater physical care and supervision required for infants.

Daycare or center-based care has a larger enrolment, children are usually grouped by age, and the environment is more like a preschool setting. Staff are typically required to have early childhood education training, ranging from a basic course up to diploma or degree level training. Staff may have additional training for specific age groups, such as infants. There will be several staff employed by the center. Daycare centers should be licensed, and many are accredited, meaning that they have met a higher standard than that of basic licensing requirements. Typically, daycare centers are licensed and approved by the government. Parents may prefer one setting over another based on the age, temperament and needs of their child. But regardless of the type of setting, there are some basics that parents should look for in a quality child care setting.

Safety: Basic safety in the setting would include child safety gates installed, electrical cords and outlets covered, cleaning supplies, implements, sharp tools and cutlery out of reach and locked away. If there is a pet, cleanliness and safety are needed. The caregiver should have certification in First Aid. The outside play spaces should be free from dangerous items and play apparatus should be in good repair. The outside area should be fenced and safe from traffic. There should be procedures in place regarding which adults can pick up the child at the end of the day. There should be smoke detectors and fire extinguishers available and in good working order.

Meals and snacks: Food served should be nutritious, fresh, and appropriate for the age of the child. Food allergies should be considered so all children are safe from exposure. There should be a minimum of highly processed foods or foods with added sugar.

Behavior guidance: The methods used to guide the children's behavior should be positive, not punitive, and based on principles of caring, positive guidance. Rules and expectations should be age-appropriate and based on values of fairness, security and safety for all the children. The caregivers and early childhood educators should interact positively with the children and show patience and caring.

Fees: Fees vary greatly. The caregiver should provide information about all costs, including whether full monthly fees are charged if a child does not attend, any additional fees for special outings, and late payment fee policy. How much notice is required if your family will be ending the child care arrangement? While the cost of child care is significant for families, don't let the fee be the main factor in your selection.

Daily activities: What goes on each day at childcare is very important. There should be activities provided that support the development of the whole child. There should be: outside active play each day; opportunities for creative play (drawing, painting or crafts); and an area and props for dramatic play (a kitchen center, dress-up clothes, doctor kit, firefighter helmet). Music should be available, both recorded music and musical instruments such as shakers, bells or drums. There should be a large supply of age-appropriate books available to the children whenever they want, as well as a story time when the caregiver reads to the children. Sensory play materials such as water, sand and playdough should be offered.

Quiet area: This is not the napping area, but a corner with soft pillows, a carpeted space and a small table with room for only one child. This allows children to have a break from the busy group activities if a child wishes to play quietly or look at books, or just be alone.

Naps and rest: The room or area where the children sleep should be comfortable with soft lighting, and the cribs, mats or playpens where the children nap should be separated by a few feet. Playpens and cribs must meet current safety requirements. Sheets and bedding should be laundered regularly, and children should have their own bedding, not using that of any other child. Mats should be cleaned and disinfected regularly. There should be some flexibility in nap or rest time, so that a child is not required to lay quietly for hours, if he no longer needs a long sleep or rest. And, there should be the opportunity to rest or sleep at a different time than the usual schedule if a child is tired.

Cleanliness and hygiene: All the children should be taught and required to wash their hands before and after eating, after using the bathroom, after coming in from playing outside, and after any messy play. Care needs to be taken that children do not share utensils or cups. With infants and toddlers, who are constantly mouthing toys, special care is needed. If a toy or item has been in a baby's mouth, it should be placed in a mild bleach solution before another infant or toddler can get it. All toys, surfaces, bathrooms and floors should be cleaned and disinfected regularly. Clear policies about ill children should be in place and followed.

The caregiver: Is the caregiver kind, empathetic and involved with the children? Does he or she seem to enjoy the children, treating each child as an individual? Is he or she positive, encouraging and patient? Is he or she well-informed about typical behaviorr of children and early childhood development? A child care provider will have a large impact on your child. In a group daycare setting, try to meet all the staff who work with your child's group, not just the director or manager. Do the staff seem happy, upbeat and enjoying their jobs? Do they smile often? Child care is not a job someone should take simply because they need a paying job—they should truly enjoy being with children. Do the staff have energy and strength or do they seem to be tired much the time? Child care is a demanding job. You want to see staff getting up and down on the floor, and easily carrying babies and toddlers.

Do the staff speak clearly to the children, using lots of words and description? Do they deliberately encourage speech development by extending words and phrases, and encouraging children to communicate? Do they get down to the child's eye level when talking? Do they read stories with expression? Is most of the conversation and communication with the children, rather than with other staff? Do they know all the children's names and use them, rather than, 'buddy' or 'baby' or other general terms? Is their focus on the children rather than doing paperwork or cleaning? Are phones used only while on breaks, not while on duty with the children? Staff should not be texting or checking their phones but focusing on the children.

Do all the children get attention from the caregiver? There should be no obvious favorites, and quieter children should still receive their share of adult time, even if they don't demand it.

When a child is upset, sad or crying, the caregiver should be sympathetic and supportive. It should be clear that the caregiver understands that crying is a way that young children communicate and responds accordingly. You should never see rough treatment, hear harsh words, or witness anger or frustration from the adults towards the children.

Staff should have training in child development, behavior guidance and programming. They should have First Aid certification. Ask if they have any other training that is pertinent to your child's needs such as a special certificate in infant care.

You will look for many of the same qualities in a family daycare home operator. While typically, a home provider is not required to have the level of formal training that a daycare staff member does, she still should have knowledge about child development which may have been gained by experience, or through workshops, self-study or courses. She should have First Aid training. Her personal qualities and skills are very important, as she will be the only adult caregiver that your child will be in contact with during the day. Some of the challenges for a family daycare home provider are the same as those of any parent at home. She needs to juggle food preparation and household tasks, while making sure the kids are supervised, busy and happy. Observe how well she multi-tasks. Be sure that the home is safe and that toys and materials suitable for older children are not in the reach of infants and toddlers. Ask to see where your child will sleep as well as the outdoor play area. Find out if there are other adults in the home who will be present when your child is there.

There is a lot to consider when selecting a caregiver, but the biggest thing is trust. Can you trust this person with your child? Can you focus on your own employment, confident that your child is safe, happy and cared for? If you have doubts, trust your gut and keep looking.

11
PARENTS NEED TO LOOK AFTER THEMSELVES

As a parent, you are the primary caregiver for your children. You have a huge responsibility and are doing probably the most important job you will ever have. Being a parent takes a lot of energy, yet unlike at a paid job, there are no scheduled breaks, lunch hours, vacation days or wellness seminars. Some parents think that taking any time for themselves is selfish, but no one can do a good job in any demanding role if they are exhausted. We all agree with that when talking about a paid job, but parents often don't see things that way when it comes to the unpaid job of parenting.

So, you might want to think about this…

Whatever airline you fly on, the safety instructions are very similar. When the flight attendant talks about placing the oxygen mask over your mouth and nose, he always says what to do if travelling with small children. Those instructions are to "Put your own mask on first", and then help the child with her oxygen mask, because the adult must be safe and healthy, in order to look after the child.

Parent self-care means to plan and take time away from your children to look after yourself. Of course, this is within reason, and there may be some parents who spend so much time on their own wants and interests that their children's needs are not met. The key is to find the balance, making sure that as a parent you can care for yourself and your adult relationships, while still mainly focusing on the important parenting role. Parents who look after themselves will have the energy, positive outlook and patience to do a better job as a parent.

Ask a group of mothers of young children what they would do if they had an hour of uninterrupted time, and you'll get a variety of responses; Take a bath, read a book, get a massage, go out for lunch…all things that provide some rejuvenation, time alone or adult contact. And you'll see a dreamy expression on many faces as the group members think about how wonderful that hour would be. Someone will usually say, "An hour! I'd like even 10 minutes!!" Asking yourself this question can help you define what it is you miss the most from the pre-parenting days, and what would give you the biggest lift. A common thing that many parents are missing is adult contact. Having the time to connect and talk with other adults is very important to avoid isolation and loneliness. Parents who find ways to get out of the house with other parents and find time for visits and phone calls with friends will feel happier and more connected. Everyone needs support and connectedness. Taking turns providing child care for each other is one good way that parents can get some time on their own. Some other ideas to help with self-care are to clear your mind with music, guided relaxation, massage, yoga or a walk or bike ride.

And don't forget to keep your body healthy. Like athletes, parents need to be on top of their game.

12
SPENDING TIME IN NATURE

If you haven't heard of the book, *Last Child in the Woods*, it might sound like a *Survivor* or *Hunger Games* kind of thing. Actually, it's a non-fiction work by Richard Louv. This award-winning book, first published in 2005, was a national bestseller and started an international movement to re-connect children and families to nature. The term "nature deficit disorder" was coined in this book to describe the decreased amount of time children spend outside in nature, which is related to many health and behavior issues. Richard Louv summarized and explained several studies that all found the same thing: being in nature is essential to a child's healthy physical and emotional development. In effect, like healthy food and water, children need to be out in nature. Think of it as "Vitamin N".

When I first read this book, I found myself thinking about pet owners. If you love dogs you'll drive great distances to take them to open spaces, to ensure they have exercise and fresh air, and you'll faithfully do this daily. Yet, a walk out in nature with children might happen only if there is time left over from the many other activities that we believe to be more important to our child's well-being.

Why is it so important to spend time outside in a natural environment? Your child gets exercise by running, climbing, jumping, crawling and balancing that happens in a natural way when you go for a walk in the woods. This helps with general health and builds strength.

Play, the key to a child's brain development, happens in a free and child-focused way. Your child learns about nature and how things grow. Being outside in fresh air helps children to sleep better. Your child will get increased Vitamin D. Increased outdoor exercise can help address childhood obesity. Being out in natural green areas reduces children's stress. (Even seeing green spaces has that positive effect.) Positive social interactions are more likely to happen when people are outside. Distance vision is improved and in some cases, the chance of a child being nearsighted decreases. Symptoms of ADHD are improved when children spend time outside.

So, how can you get "Vitamin N" for your child? Check out your local community hiking trails, conservation areas, woods and fields. If you don't have much time, go to the local park or playground. But try to look for natural areas and fields. Talk to your child about what you both are seeing and doing. Encourage exploration.

Children who play outside are happier and healthier. Parents see this, and research has confirmed it. And it doesn't cost anything to get outside-there's no uniforms, equipment, or registration fees!

13
PLAYTIME FOR PRESCHOOLERS

We know that young children learn best from hands-on involvement with real concrete things, not from passive activities such as screen watching. We should encourage our children to play, not just watch. Tablets, TV and other devices keep young children occupied but there are better ways for kids to spend their free time.

Play includes such things as using the senses (water, sand, play dough), toy cars and other things that go, dramatic play (dressing up, playing 'house'), building with blocks and other construction materials, playing with dolls or toy animals and painting or drawing. It also includes games and active physical play.

Play helps in all areas of child development. Playing shouldn't just be something that children get to do when there is a bit of extra free time. Play is how children learn, grow and develop. Play allows for exercise and physical activity, language development, social interaction and use of imagination. The complicated dramatic play that children can create is wonderful to see. They pretend to cook, serve a meal, look after dolls, dress up to get ready for work, build or repair things, deliver mail or newspapers, all with props that are easily found around your home and incorporated into the play area.

Many children have very busy schedules, with music lessons, sports and other activities that well-meaning parents enroll them in. While there is nothing wrong with these activities, parents should make sure that there is lots of time for free play, too. Free play is fun, chosen and controlled by the child, and it's not focused on an end result. It allows for creativity and imagination.

Some parents think they will help their child to succeed in school by limiting free play time and have their children spend much more time on activities such as flash card learning, educational shows, educational computer games or structured lessons in a variety of activities. This is understandable, but misguided. As parents, we want to encourage the intellectual development of our kids, but research shows that children learn best from hands-on, interactive, concrete experiences. And we need to remember that the whole child needs nurturing, not just the intellectual area. Many of the things children learn while they play are skills we take for granted as adults but are highly important to successful adult life, such as how to plan, share, problem-solve, wait, recognize how others are feeling, explain, create, deal with frustration and take turns.

Parents can make sure there is a play time each day for their children. If they seem bored with their toys, don't seem to know how to start playing, and typically prefer to turn on the tablet or television, ask yourself if you have the toys and activities available that encourage free play.

What should you have in your home to encourage free play? Many parent educators and early childhood professionals recommend having the following items in your home for lots of play value, scope for imagination, and hours of fun and creative play:

    Blocks
    Balls
    Art supplies such as crayons, paints, tape, glue
    Cars and other vehicles
    Dolls and accessories
    Stuffed animals and puppets
    Puzzles
    Small figures of people and animals
    Dress-up clothes and role-playing props
    Musical instruments such as drums, shakers, harmonicas, bells
    Cardboard boxes
    Books
    Cards and card games
    Board games
    Water and sand and tools for filling, pouring and digging

Avoid noisy toys, which can be harmful to hearing. Also avoid battery-operated toys which at first are very attractive and interesting to a child, but then are unused once the novelty is gone.

With the time to play and lots of materials to be play with, you shouldn't hear, "There's nothing to do," very often. And don't forget to include lots of outdoor active play in your family routine as well.

14
GETTING THE KIDS TO PLAY OUTSIDE

Parents often say, "It's nice out—how about playing outside?" But kids often do not want to go out. Why do they seem to get bored quickly and prefer to come back in, probably to watch television or play video games?

For good physical and emotional health, everyone (adults and children) should get outside each day. For kids, outside play has many benefits: fresh air; physical activity; development of motor skills; and a chance to be noisy and to use their imaginations.

Here are some ideas to help your child enjoy being outside:

Collections: Help your child get organized to start a collection—it doesn't matter what, rocks, leaves, wood. Set up a box or shelf where they can keep their treasures.

Gardening: Give a section of the yard or flowerbed or get some containers for your child's own garden. Let them shop with you to buy seeds. Be sure to select some fast growing, interesting things, such as beans. Help them to plant, then show them how to water and weed. They will want to check and tend their garden frequently.

Photography: Let your child take pictures of things outside and share them with you. Ask them questions like, "Why did you choose to take a picture of that? What was interesting to you?" They can take pictures of flowers, bugs, birds and their growing garden. Let them print some of the photos they like the best and keep an album or scrapbook.

Go for a daily walk or bike ride with your child: Safety concerns in many communities mean that you can't send your kids out alone to do this, so make the time to go along. You will feel better, too!

Birds and other local wildlife: Encourage an interest in local birds and animals. Get books about birds and look at pictures. Get your child to take pictures and to use binoculars to watch them. Make a counting game out of spotting birds and keep a daily total of how many birds your child sees.

Bugs: Kids usually find insects very interesting. Get a child-safe magnifying glass and let your child explore bugs up close.

Sidewalk chalk: This is lots of fun for kids. Show them how to play hopscotch. Give pails of water and a scrub brush to 'erase' the chalk. Draw roads and racetracks and then have running races.

Play 'going camping': Set up a tent outside, or even just blankets over boxes or chairs. Bring out sleeping bags, play food, dishes or a play kitchen. Kids love to hang out in tents.

Water play: On hot days set up the sprinkler and run, run, run! Give the kids paint brushes and buckets of water and let them 'paint' the fence. On certain days, when you have the energy to clean them up afterwards, let kids make mud pies using the garden hose.

Sand play: If possible, have a sand box in your yard. Keep it covered when not in use to keep out animals and to keep it clean. Buckets, toy vehicles, rakes and shovels will provide hours of fun. Kids love to build a town with buildings and make roads between their structures. If you can only use sand at the playground, consider taking along some large jugs of water. Dry sand is not nearly as fun as wet sand!

Group games: Organize a play date so there are enough kids to play these old-fashioned games. Teach them to play Tag, Frozen Tag, Kick the Can, Statues, Follow the Leader. Set up relay races. These encourage running, jumping and the development of large motor skills. Older kids really enjoy flag football. You can use old scarves or ties as the flags and a softer round ball, (rather than a football) to make it easier. Another game kids really enjoy is kickball (just like baseball except using a larger bouncy ball) with the 'batter' simply kicking the ball, and then running to first base.

Have a picnic: This doesn't have to be an elaborate picnic at a park. Just do snack time or lunch time outside as often as possible when the weather is good. You can all sit on a blanket; let the kids help prepare the food, and then pour and serve drinks. You can make homemade juice popsicles together the day before and then enjoy them outside while dripping anywhere.

Go to the playground: If you find that your kids go on the apparatus briefly and then get bored, try a game of Tag or Follow the Leader. Try imaginative play by acting out a favorite story. For example, Jack and the Beanstalk can be used to encourage the kids to climb up, tiptoe and then run to a designated place to be 'safe' when the giant wakes up. You can be the giant. Or pretend all the ground is water and no one should get wet, encouraging lots of climbing and swinging on the apparatus.

If you model how much fun it is to play outside, and use your imagination to get your kids engaged, they will have a great time. Soon they will take the lead in outside play, using their own creative ideas.

15
YOUNG CHILDREN AND QUIET TIMES

In our busy, noisy and crowded lives, it can be difficult to find space and time for quiet time alone. Yet this is something that everyone needs, including children. Children often spend large amounts of time in group settings; school, organized sports, daycare, stores—even home can be a busy, noisy and crowded place. In these settings, children are required to wait, share, be cooperative and interact with many people. Constant social interaction can create stress in children, which can lead to inappropriate behavior, conflict or withdrawal. Some children seem to have little need for quiet time, while others have a greater need. These differences in temperament are neither right nor wrong. Never label a child as shy, timid or intense. A more outgoing child may not be aware that he is over-stimulated or becoming frustrated until a 'meltdown' takes place. Everyone can benefit from a quiet pause in the day. Here are some suggestions for providing quiet, private spaces for children:

Provide earphones, taped stories, and music.

Make sure there is a place—a cupboard, closet, or drawer where your child can keep his own things and special possessions, safe from siblings and other children.

Try to make nap or rest time in the same quiet and restful room each day—not a quick nap in the car or on a couch. Favorite blankets or stuffed animals help make this a pleasant break in the day.

Have books accessible in a quiet corner with cushions or quilts to make a 'nest'. You might want to keep some special books put away and bring them out to encourage interest. You can also keep photo albums in this area—children really enjoy looking at the pictures.

Never use the quiet corner or area as a time-out place or discipline technique.

Puzzles, a special pop-up book, markers and large paper can be placed at a small table or area that is out of the way of activities. You can make a surprise box, and fill it with small toys, beads, cards, etc. and offer this to your child at certain times to encourage quiet, individual activity.

Have a no-interruption rule in your family for certain situations. In the same way that an adult may need to be at the computer or desk to complete certain tasks, allow a child to choose to be alone and uninterrupted. A child who is involved in a book or activity should not always have to share or take turns.

Give young children a few warnings if you do have to end their quiet play time. For example, say, "We have to go shopping in 10 minutes", And then later say, "We have to leave soon." You may need to promise that no one will touch the things the child has been playing with while you are gone.

Create a play tent or fort from large pillows and blankets. This will encourage imaginary games and act as a sanctuary from noise and people.

Turn off the TV and screens. Constant background sound can be stressful for many people. Do not have a

TV or device in your child's bedroom. And screens don't work as a tool for quiet times. The noise and stimulation have been shown to interfere with sleep patterns in children.

Be a model for your child, by taking your own quiet moments to recharge. Explain to your child what you are doing and why, saying something like, "Let's have some quiet time." Let your child see you enjoying quiet time with electronics turned off.

Try some of these suggestions to reduce stress and you may find that your child is calmer and happier.

16
WHAT DOES SCHOOL SUCCESS MEAN TO YOU?

We all want our kids to succeed at school but let's consider what we mean by success. Do we want our child to be a straight-A student, star athlete, respected and liked by teachers? Do we hope our child will be popular, or a leader at student council? Or do we hope that our child will be kind, helpful and supportive to others?

As a parent, it's important to know what you consider success to be. The goal of schooling is to help children to prepare for adult life and to thrive in their lives. To accomplish this, your child will need to learn skills in more than the academic areas. Of course, you want them to be academically successful, but we also need to think about physical development, social skills and emotional maturity including empathy, creativity and spiritual development. If your child has straight As, that's great, but is she also developing in the other areas? If your child is athletically gifted, and very successful in school sports, does he also have opportunities to develop his creative skills?

What would you do in this situation? A young teen in Grade 8 named Ryan is identified by his teachers as being academically gifted and is invited to attend a special academic program offered at another school. Ryan currently has a large positive group of friends, is active in sports and other extracurricular activities and is involved in student leadership and volunteer events at the school. What is the best decision for this young teen? The parents, John and Kristin, discussed this academic opportunity with Ryan and his teachers considering the benefits of the special program, and the potential pitfalls. To make a good decision, John and Kristin needed to be clear on what they considered school success for Ryan to be.

In this situation, the parents (and Ryan) decided not to move to the special academic program. John and Kristin were particularly happy with Ryan's peers and did not want to jeopardize those positive relationships. Was this the best decision? There are so many variables that they will never know for sure, but Ryan grew up to be a well-rounded, educated and employed adult with a good relationship with his parents. In their decision, John and Kristin considered school to be the support for the development of the whole person, not just the means for learning academic subject matter. Success in school for this family meant the development of their child in all areas.

So, as parents support their children to be successful in school, take the time to be clear about what you think success really means.

17
BE INVOLVED WITH YOUR CHILD'S SCHOOL

As parents, we hope our child will be successful at school, learning and growing towards adulthood and independence. Children spend many hours in school, and parents can help make this time successful by trying the following tips.

Read aloud daily and have conversations with your child. Sometimes as our children get older, we may no longer think reading aloud is as important, but it is still a special and valuable way to spend time with your child, building vocabulary and lifelong learning skills. Asking your child to read aloud to you using "chapter books" is a great way to help with fluency in reading. Encourage general conversation with open-ended questions like, "What was a good thing about your day at school?" Or, you can ask your children to think of a topic of conversation to raise at the supper table, such as a current event, an upcoming trip, or a sports event, a movie or a book.

Get to know your child's teachers. Recognize that school success is a team effort from teachers and parents. Encourage and support the teachers' efforts.

Get involved at the school. Volunteer in the classroom, sign up for excursions or help with fund raising. Attend concerts and plays. Attend parent-teacher conferences, even if you have no major concerns. This sends a message to your child that school is important and allows you to be aware of what's going on at school. Another benefit is getting to know your child's peers and other parents, building a community of supports.

Make learning a priority in your family. Children and adults alike are constantly learning. With the rapid rate of change in technology and knowledge in our society, we all need to read, look up information, learn new skills and follow current events. Modelling the importance of learning will help your children value their own schools and education.

Limit screen time. Children need time to think, create, play and be physically active to learn. Be sure that screen time is not dominating your lives.

Teach your children that work comes before play. Schoolwork comes before free time. And household chores or other responsibilities come before fun activities. There may be some exceptions because of family schedules, but you want your children to realize that real life works this way. You can't just NOT do a task because you don't feel like it.

Have a regular, uninterrupted, quiet homework time: It's best to also have a dedicated location—a desk or table where homework is done.

Compliment your kids when they have a good idea, solve a problem or make an effort. Don't praise only for top grades or for being the best. Focus on the attempts and progress your child is making.

Resist the temptation to do your child's homework for them. Offer to help when they have a problem, but don't take over.

If you have a concern about your child's learning, set up a phone call or face-to-face meeting with the teacher. Remember that you both have the same goal; for your child to be happy and successful in school. Work together to develop positive solutions to the issue.

Don't just focus on grades. Avoid being overly critical and don't expect perfection. As with all parenting skills and interactions with your children, be positive and caring.

18
WHAT A HIGH SCHOOL TEACHER WOULD LIKE PARENTS TO KNOW

I talked with a high school teacher (I'll call him Mark) about how parents can support their teens as they attend school. We discussed many of the usual topics—encouraging completing assignments, punctuality and being involved with school activities. Then I asked, "Is there something you would like to see change about the way some parents are about their teen's teachers?"

Some very interesting points emerged in the conversation. Mark noted that some teachers are better than others at delivering information and ensuring the students have effective learning opportunities. Some are better at developing positive relationships with their students. But for the most part, teachers truly care about their students. It is not a battle between parents and teachers. Parents have their role and teachers have theirs. Both are united in the same educational goal, helping the student learn. Teachers respect the role of parents and parents need to respect the role of the teacher.

Mark gave some examples of parents who accept without question what their teen tells them about school. These parents may believe that this unconditional acceptance of information is good parenting, because it is showing unconditional support for their child. He recommends that if parents don't agree with something a teacher is doing or are told by their child about a situation that they find concerning, that the parent should contact the school for more information and a discussion about the situation. Do not just immediately accept without question that their child's opinion or description of what goes on in the classroom is accurate. This is not to imply that the student is lying, but the student may not know the entire situation, may have misunderstood, or may not be willing to admit they have behaved inappropriately. There are two sides to every story.

When there is a difference of opinion between the teacher and the student, or when a teen complains about the teacher, parents should not immediately agree with their child, and should not allow a critical or insulting conversation with their teen about the teacher. Instead, parents can focus on constructive ways to deal with the situation. Mark told me that some students roll their eyes, speak rudely, interrupt their teachers or refuse reasonable requests. If these disrespectful behaviors are allowed at home, with parents allowing insulting, critical comments to be made about the teachers, (or even joining in with disrespectful comments) then it is no wonder that the students behave this way at school.

He also pointed out that if the goal of education is to prepare students for adult life, then parents who side with their children without question are not doing their kids any favours. As adults, we work with and talk with people we might not like very much and whose opinions we may disagree with. Using basic courtesy and having respectful interactions even when we disagree is a key to successful adult life. As well, most adults have had a supervisor or manager who runs things in a way they don't support. As an employee, you still must follow that manager's instructions (or be fired).

So, this high school teacher would like parents to know that supporting your child is important, but that this does not mean *unconditional* support.

I thought about my conversation with Mark and came to this conclusion. Since none of our children is perfect at home, it's not likely that they are perfect at school. As parents, we can all keep this in mind and work as partners with teachers for our children's success and well-being.

19
CONNECTING WITH KIDS

How was school? Fine. What did you do? Nothing. Trying to show an interest in your kids to connect with them can become more difficult as they get older. Verbal interactions often take the form of directions, commands or reminders rather than real conversations. Think about the time you spent with your children in the past few days. Did you have a one-on-one conversation with each child? Was it an actual conversation or was it—

    Do you have your backpack?
    Don't forget we have gymnastics right after school.
    Are your dirty dishes in the dishwasher?
    Shut off the TV! (tablet or phone).
    Supper's ready.

Here are some ideas for connecting with kids through real conversation. First of all, keep in mind your tone of voice and volume. Would you start a conversation with another adult in the way you are speaking to your child? Even with reminders or directions, do you remember to say please and thank you to your child? Do you use a tone of request, rather than one of command? Do you avoid criticism and nagging in the same way that you would with another adult? It's strange that many people are more polite and patient with acquaintances than with the family members that they love.

Another way to encourage conversation to connect is to use creative questions. Instead of "How was school?" try, "Did you do anything new today at school?" or specific questions like, "Is the class still learning decimals in Math? What books or poems are you reading? Which book or poem did you like? What sport are you doing in PE this week?" Volunteer information about your own day.

Conversation can flow more easily when it's not the entire focus. To prevent a conversation being awkward or stilted, start it when you are doing something together, such as clearing the table, watering the garden or emptying the dishwasher. Ask your child to set the table or do some other task in the kitchen while you are preparing a meal. Do a craft activity together, go for a walk or work on a project.

Many parents find that bed time is when their child starts a lengthy conversation, often about something that is worrying them. If this is the case at your home, be sure to be fully present and attentive. The timing may not be the best right before sleep time, but when your child initiates a conversation you need to respond and give them the time they need to talk.

Try your best to have family meal times together. It's nearly impossible to sit down together for breakfast or lunch on week days but make a point of having supper as a family around a table as often as you can. Families connect around a shared meal. No phones, TV or other devices allowed. You can try having some conversational topics ready. Some parents suggest, "Everyone tell me two things that were good about today, and one thing that was not so good." Parents should participate in this too. Even if your children try to eat quickly and get away from the table, insist that everyone is together at the table for a set amount of time, even if it's ten minutes. As conversation become longer and more interesting, you may find that the 'supper hour' becomes a full hour, with lively conversation, sharing and debate.

20
POSITIVE CONVERSATIONS WITH TEENS

As children enter the teen years, a lot can change. Puzzled parents may feel that they are living with a distant acquaintance—a confused, self-absorbed, impulsive and over-sensitive houseguest. So, how can you get along better with your teen?

Remind yourself that teens go through a lot during those years. Young teens have rapid gains in height and weight and rapid brain development, as they physically mature into adults. They require more sleep and may seem clumsy as they get accustomed to their new body size and shape. Emotional and behavioral changes take place. Parents may notice their teen's rapid mood swings, impulsiveness and a belief that he or she is invincible, which can lead to risky behaviors. Younger teens or preteens will behave differently than 14 or 15-year-olds, who will be different from 17 or 18-year-olds. And although 18 years may be the age of legal adulthood, older teens can still use some gentle guidance from their parents. It can all be difficult for parents but think how challenging these years are for teens! In addition to the changes taking place, many teens feel pressured, stressed, worried, lonely and incredibly self-conscious, as if they are being watched and judged about everything, all the time. How can a parent help?

Although sometimes it may not seem like it, teens do appreciate their families and need to be connected. Some parents might pull back in an effort to give their teen the autonomy and 'space' they seem to want. Yet, teens need their parents, and generally do appreciate them, although they might not show it in obvious ways. Here are some suggestions from teens as to what they wish their parents would do (and not do):

Listen. Don't freak out and immediately offer solutions and advice.

Ask what she thinks is fun.

Recognize that he is growing up.

Stay calm and don't overreact.

Treat her as a unique individual.

Let go of past mistakes and don't bring them up at every occasion.

Don't talk about him when he is present, as if he isn't there. (It doesn't matter if the comments are negative or positive.)

Don't tell stories about when she was little or repeat embarrassing anecdotes.

Don't say he is too young to understand or to make a decision.

Don't say, "You'll live, you'll get over it," or any comment that belittles her concerns.

Don't say, "I know what you mean. I went through the same thing and it turned out okay."

Don't always talk about school or sports achievement.

Don't focus on the negative, on the things he didn't do. Don't say, "we only want you to try your best," but then be disappointed by the outcome.

Don't use sarcasm.

Don't compare her to other teens or siblings.

Don't get upset when he wants to spend less time with parents and family or wants to be alone.

Here are some phrases suggested by parent educators that parents can try using to have a positive conversation with teenagers. They won't guarantee peace, but they are a start to building and maintaining a positive relationship. Try saying:

- Do you want some ideas to fix the problem or do you want me to just listen?

- How can I help?

- I'd like to understand you a little better. Would you tell me your ideas about—?

- I don't know much about this, but I would like to help in any way that I can.

So when your teenager starts a conversation, be sure to be available. Respond to them calmly and let them know you care. Try not to judge. The way you respond should always send the message, "I care about you and I want to help."

21
SPANKING

Child abuse sadly is not uncommon in our country. A 2014 study published in the Canadian Medical Association Journal found that 33 per cent of Canadians had experienced physical abuse, sexual abuse, exposure to violence in the home, spanking with an object or slapping. These types of experiences were found to have a strong correlation with mental disorders, including suicidal thoughts and suicidal attempts.

One risk factor for child abuse is found in parents who have a strong belief in corporal punishment. These parents believe physical punishment will control their child's behavior. But if parents are under stress due to employment or family factors, they are at risk of going too far with their children. They may become enraged and out of control, inflicting physical injury or even death on their children. Tragically, even infants have been victims of out-of-control adults.

People who would be horrified at anyone physically injuring a child may feel that physical punishment such as spanking is a completely different thing. But spanking also has been shown to have long-term harmful effects on children. Children who are spanked as kids are more likely to be physically aggressive with other kids, and as adults, more likely to use violence to deal with conflict with their spouses or their own children.

Worldwide, over sixty countries prohibit corporal punishment. In Canada and the United States, spanking is not illegal. Legal or not, there are far better ways to guide and discipline children, ways that are more effective and do not harm children. Parents can learn these methods from programs offered at family centers in your community, or from online programs. (Be sure the programs are from a reliable source.)

So why do parents spank their children, if it is risky and harmful to kids? The simple answer is that on the surface, and in the short term, it appears that spanking works because it stops the behavior at that moment. Unfortunately, this reinforces parents in their belief that spanking is a good method for changing the actions of a child. What is not so immediately obvious is that more frequent, or increasingly harsher physical punishment is needed to have the same effect. As well, the child who behaves through fear of pain is not learning anything about self-control, self-discipline or empathy. Do parents want a child who becomes a teenager and adult who only behaves when they are afraid they might get caught and hurt? And, as the child gets older, it will not be physically possible to spank them, and so then what will a parent do? Punishment can create resentment and children may seek revenge by doing something much worse than the original action. Spanking models aggression and violence, sending a message that a larger, stronger person can do what they want to those smaller and weaker. In any other context we would consider this bullying or assault. In my opinion, spanking is just another word for hitting.

Some parents spank because they don't know what else to do. Parenting education can provide the skills and techniques to discipline children in a positive, harm-free way that builds relationships, mutual respect and self-discipline. It's notable that the Canadian Paediatric Society strongly discourages physical punishment including spanking. The American Academy of Pediatrics also opposes striking a child for any reason. We all need to accept that spanking can harm your child emotionally and, in some cases, can lead to physical harm or abuse. Here are some suggestions for disciplining without spanking.

Take away privileges. For example, computer games, use of a bike, movies. It's best if the consequences are logical and linked to the undesirable behavior. So, if the child refuses to turn off their tablet and come for supper, she would lose the privilege of using the tablet for a set period of time. If the child doesn't lock up his bike, he would not be allowed to ride it for a period of days. If the child is playing too roughly or being unkind to younger siblings, he would not be allowed to play for a few minutes.

Allow the child to experience the natural consequences of her behavior if it is safe and appropriate to do so. The natural consequence of running up to a strange dog might be to get bitten, so of course you would not allow that to happen. But leaving their belongings or toys all over, instead of putting them away when asked, might mean they can't be found when the child wants them. The natural consequence would be that they can't play with that item, or wear those shoes, as a natural result of their own behavior. Don't pitch in to help find the item.

Have age appropriate expectations. Be sure you are not expecting too much of a young child. Many parents aren't sure of the typical age of developmental readiness to manage certain behaviors, such as eating neatly, sitting quietly or not talking. It's simply not fair to discipline a child for something they are not yet capable of doing. I remember seeing a parent scolding a two-year-old in a restaurant for not being able to sit quietly at the table and wait for the food. This is an unrealistic expectation. Expecting a two-year-old to share is an unreasonable expectation. Sharing well with others is possible between age three and a half to four. Expecting a three-year-old to clean up all her toys is unreasonable. She can certainly help, and will do some of the tasks, but should not be disciplined when she doesn't complete the job as an adult would. Expecting a three-year-old to sit through a movie at the theatre is also unrealistic. After paying the admission, purchasing snacks, and settling in, parents are dismayed if after 15 minutes their child starts standing up, kicking seats and wandering in the aisle. Again, the child should not be punished for this. The self-control needed to sit still and quietly for over an hour is not yet developed.

Make it easy for your child to behave by removing temptations. For example, a toddler is going to try to go down or up the stairs, no matter what you say, or how many times you move her away. Get a baby gate. Keep special or breakable items out of reach. Keep your phone out of sight if you don't want your kids playing with it.

"Time-out" is a discipline technique that creates a lot of strong opinions, both for and against. Time-out means taking the child away from the area and not giving him any attention for a short period of time. My view is that it is far preferable to spanking, and if done properly, does not shame or harm the child. Time-out should be a brief break from the situation and does not include parents shouting at or shaming the child.

Try different discipline techniques as an alternative to the harmful practice of spanking

22
AVOID NEGATIVE BEHAVIOR BEFORE IT STARTS

The challenging task of successful parenting often centers on kids' behavior. Parents attend groups and seek help when their kids won't behave. The bad behavior is often due to stress that the child is experiencing—behavior is a way of communicating. The frequency of problems can be reduced if you think about *preventing* challenging behavior, rather than reacting to it. One easy tip to help children deal with stress and self-control is to use the acronym HALT. HALT stands for Hungry, Angry, Lonely, Tired.

Parents, ask yourself: Is it possible that my child is hungry? Even adults with mature self-control can get irritable and impatient when we are hungry. So, it's that much more difficult for a child to control his emotions if he's hungry. Children need to eat frequently with several small nutritious meals and snacks per day. Eating five or six times per day is appropriate for toddlers and preschoolers. Often, children don't realize they are hungry, so every two hours or so, offer a nutritious snack. Don't forget about water—we often need water before our bodies tell us that we feel thirsty.

A is for Angry. Has your child had a disappointment or been frustrated? Think about what has been going on in the recent past, remembering that what might seem minor to an adult can be very important to a child. Talk to your child about how they are feeling and why.

L is for Lonely. Children who feel that they are not getting enough attention or who have been alone a lot will often seek attention in negative ways. For a child, negative attention is preferable to no attention at all. Demands, crying, tantrums and sibling conflict can often be prevented by offering a child your undivided attention. You can offer to play a game, read a story, color a picture or do a craft. Offer to go outside and play together. Let your child choose the activity and take the lead. Try to spend time with your child, *before* he demands your attention in negative ways.

T is for Tired. Just as parents may have a bad day after a late night or restless night's sleep, so do children. And children are less able to control their behavior than adults are. Kids need a LOT of sleep. Preschoolers ages three to five need on average 10 to 13 hours per day and children ages six to 12 need nine to 12 hours. Children will rarely say they are tired, but instead will become irritable, whiny or over-active.

So if you find yourself frequently reacting to your child's challenging behavior, think of HALT. Consider whether a nap or rest, a snack, or some positive attention will solve the behavior challenge. This is a loving and positive way to help your child. Try to prevent the behavior by being aware of your child's needs and meeting them before problems happen.

23
DEALING WITH THE WORST TIME OF DAY FOR FAMILY STRESS

Parenting is stressful, and parents need to make a deliberate effort to manage stress in order to be successful parents. There are many ways that parents can take care of themselves and manage their own stress, providing children with the most supportive environment possible. One important thing to do is to get your home and routine organized.

Think about certain times of day that you find are the most stressful or chaotic. For many of us, it's the morning rush—trying to get everyone to have breakfast, make school lunches, organize backpacks and have everyone on their way in time for school or work. If the mornings are typically filled with arguments, demands, frantic searching for a parent permission form or required item for school, shoes or jacket, then it's time to get organized.

The easiest way to address the morning chaos is to do as much as possible night before. Get the lunches made, pack the backpacks, have the next day's clothes, shoes and jackets laid out for the morning. To avoid tears and meltdowns, check that all homework and school items are done. If you and your children get this done before a bedtime snack and story, you'll find the next day much less stressful.

Another tough time of day for parents is just before supper. Everyone is tired from their day at school, daycare or work, and everyone is hungry. Patience can wear thin. These suggestions might help.

Have nutritious snacks on hand to help bridge the time until supper. Allow time for everyone to wind down, without too many demands. Try to keep your home fairly quiet at this time. Children (and adults) may need some alone time doing a quiet activity without anyone bothering them, but often children don't realize that they've been over-stimulated and need this quiet time. Try to set up routines of quieter, solitary activities if this is what your children seem to need. Encourage coloring, drawing and craft time, by having a small desk or table available with crayons, markers, glue sticks, stickers, coloring books and lots of paper. Jigsaw puzzles are helpful for encouraging quiet, focused time. Have puzzles set out. Looking at books and reading are always restful. Set out books for your kids, rather than having them all on a bookshelf. This will help them to choose to sit and read or look at books.

If your child has spent a long time that day sitting still, (in school, on the bus or in your car on a long commute), she might need physical activity, not quiet time. Music and dancing, exercising, running games like tag or follow the leader, any outside play, may be what is needed after a long day at daycare or school.

If you are a two-adult family or have older teens or other relatives living in your home, decide who is on duty with the kids during busy times. During a busy stage of life with our three preschoolers, I'd ask my husband, 'Do you want to be on kids, or on chores?' We decided who was in charge of everything to do with the kids for the next hour or so, which allowed the other person to quickly complete the cooking, tidying or other household tasks. This really reduced the stress; chores were completed without interruption or worrying about what the kids were up to. The adult who was 'on kid duty' took care of any requests, arguments, tears or accidents. It was a division of labour that really helped us manage.

Try to identify the toughest, most stressful times of day in your family routine. Some small changes can make a big difference for you and your children.

24
HELPING YOUR CHILD TO BE RESPECTFUL

Respect is a word that we hear often. Phrases like "Show some respect," or "Respect your elders", were commonly said by adults to children in the past. Similar statements are still heard today, especially in a home with an authoritarian style of parenting. The implication is that children should automatically show respect to all adults and those in positions of authority, such as teachers, caregivers or coaches.

But in our society, this is no longer the case—we hear children are more disrespectful than in the past. Whether this is accurate or not, it's not reasonable to expect children to show respect if they have not experienced it.

Those statements also assume that children know what showing respect looks like, that they know which actions and words actually are being respectful. Parents and other adults need to *teach* children what respect looks like. Ask yourself if respect has been modelled in your household. Has the child seen and heard consistent examples of respectful interactions? One way to determine if you are doing this is to really listen to yourself when speaking to your child. Do you show respect to them? If you're not sure, ask yourself if you would speak to a friend, co-worker or other acquaintance in the way you speak to your child. Of course, you will need to correct or guide your child, but this can be done in a respectful way. Here are some examples:

"Could you please turn down the music, I'm on the phone and can't hear very well."

This is how you would ask another adult, instead of yelling, "Turn down that noise!"

"Please slow down, I'm worried that something will get knocked over and break. Running games are for outside."

Instead of "Don't be so stupid." Or, "I've told you over and over not to do that."

Again, would you speak to a co-worker that way when they make mistakes?

None of us has perfect parenting skills, and if you do find yourself speaking or acting disrespectfully to your child, apologize and identify what is was that was disrespectful. For example, "I'm sorry I didn't listen to what you were trying to say to me. That wasn't very respectful. I'd like you to tell me again, because I really want to hear about it."

Even with the best of examples from adults, children will need some coaching and guidance from adults. One of the first steps is to teach basic manners to your child.

Teach them to say, "please", "thank you", and "excuse me". Explain to them that name-calling is not allowed. And of course, parents need to make sure they are doing the same. When a child does act in a disrespectful way, calm correction should be your response. For example, "We don't say 'Shut Up' to people. Please do not say that. It's not respectful. What's another way you can ask him to be quieter?" Give your child the words to say if necessary.

Another example is, "I don't talk to you that way and I don't want you to talk to me that way. It's not respectful. Can you ask me again in a respectful way?"

In our society, people are very sensitive to signs of disrespect and may react with anger or even violence. In order to help our children to get along with others, build positive relationships and avoid dangerous confrontations, our parenting role needs to include helping children to treat others with respect.

25
UNDERSTANDING YOUR CHILD'S TEMPERAMENT

I remember a friend telling me that if her third baby had been her first, she might not have had more than one child. That rueful statement was related to the temperament of her third child, which was much more challenging than the calm, easy-going natures of the first two. It can be a surprise to parents how different siblings can be in temperament.

For parents who are trying to use positive parenting strategies to be the best parents they can, it's crucial to understand your child's temperament. Temperament describes a child's typical way of responding to the world. It appears that temperament is genetically based, but of course is then modified by the environment, including the type of parenting experienced.

Some kids are just naturally quiet, calm and more reserved while others are outgoing, talkative and loud. Some are generally easy-going, "go with the flow" types, while others are strong-willed and resistant to change. Children with temperaments that parents find challenging are often called "spirited" children. Children fall somewhere along a continuum with their individual traits. Taking some time to think about and understand the facets of a child's temperament can be helpful for parents. It will help a parent to anticipate reactions, avoid conflicts and help a child with his own self-control.

There is no temperament that is better than another; what really matters is being aware of how your child fits into your home environment and how she aligns with your own ways of being. If you and your child have very different temperaments, it can be challenging to keep things on an even keel. You might not realize how difficult certain situations can be for your child.

Here's an example. Many children have trouble with new situations. If you as a parent are very adaptable, jumping right into new situations and challenges, it might be difficult to understand why your child holds back from a fun activity, doesn't want to try new things and refuses to do something, despite your reassurances and the opportunity to see that other kids are doing it. So as a parent, you have some choices—you can plead, argue, reason or even insist that your child participate. Or, you can realize that the situation looks very different to him than it does to you and let your child decide when he is ready. I remember seeing a parent lift her young daughter up on a pony, despite the child's insistence that she didn't want to. The parent knew there was no danger from the gentle pony, all the other preschoolers had taken a turn, but for this child, it was a scary, unpleasant and stressful experience. Not surprisingly, the little girl began to cry and fuss.

One of the key factors in a child's temperament is intensity. This describes how strong your child's emotional reactions are, how easily he becomes frustrated, and how strongly he reacts. A child with high intensity would get frustrated easily and have strong emotional responses. Parents may find themselves puzzled and frustrated when their child reacts strongly, thinking "it's not a big deal." Knowing that your child is of high intensity will help parents anticipate and modify situations that will be a challenge for their child.

Another factor is sensitivity. Some children are very aware of noise, smells, taste, temperature and texture. Children who are highly sensitive may be unable to stand scratchy clothes, refuse to wear a certain pair of shoes, complain of smells, or be unable to eat food with a certain texture. If you are a parent who has low sensitivity to noise, smell, and textures, then you might think your child is just being "picky". Or, you might think your child is being deliberately difficult. Instead, try to understand and empathize with your sensitive child.

Being aware of your child's temperament can help children and parents avoid many behavioral challenges. However, if you have a concern that your child is extremely intense or sensitive you should consult a health professional for an assessment.

26
SHOULD PARENTS MAKE THEIR KIDS SAY "I'M SORRY"?

Let's look at the goals behind having your child say, "I'm sorry". An apology is not meant to be an excuse or a way to get "off the hook." The goal behind an apology is to repair relationships, accept responsibility for something and make a commitment to not do that again. Without that understanding, the word "sorry" has little meaning. It's not the saying of the words that matter, but the meaning behind them.

Most parents can get their child to obey the command to "Say you're sorry!" through removal of privileges or other consequences, but there no meaning in those words being spoken if the child is only saying it so the parent will stop nagging or hold back on unpleasant consequences. Forcing children to make an apology might even make a child angrier and more resentful. Some children say the words only because of fear of punishment and might not even realize that they did something wrong.

Older children—those who haven't understood the meaning of a true apology—can be heard saying in an outraged tone, "I *said* I'm sorry," as if that makes everything okay again and their previous behavior is justified. They believe that "I'm sorry" is like a magic phrase that allows them to do whatever they want, as long as they quickly say the phrase afterward. Other children will refuse to apologize for accidental actions, because they mistakenly believe that apologies are only if they did something on purpose. They may refuse to say, "I'm sorry", using the justification, "it was an accident!" or "I didn't mean to!" How can parents help children learn about apologizing?

Learning how to apologize can start when your child is very young. We've all seen a toddler grab a toy they want from another child. Their thoughts seem to be: "I like that, I want that, I don't have it, how can I get it? I'll grab it." This is totally normal and unsurprising at this age. (It actually is basic problem-solving.) Thoughts of fairness, sharing and ownership don't enter the toddler's mind— those concepts need to be learned and practiced. They develop with maturity and guidance. In that situation, a well-meaning parent might take the toy back, return it to the first child and insist that the toddler say 'Sorry'. But without any other actions or words, the toddler will not learn from this experience. 'Sorry' is meaningless if the child doesn't know what it was they did that was wrong or hurtful. In this situation, a parent could say something like, "Jack, look at Emma. She's upset because she was using that toy that you took". The parent can then have Jack give the toy back to Emma and say, "Jack, you can have a turn later". Model the apology by saying, "We are sorry that Jack grabbed that from you. He forgot to ask if he could have a turn."

Model how to apologize as situations arise; your children will notice. And when required, apologize to your kids. Apologizing to a child is not giving up parental authority or giving in; it is treating a child with the respect that you would give any other person. An example might be, "I'm sorry that I didn't pay attention when you were showing me that picture. I got distracted. I really want to see it." This apology accepts responsibility, tries to repair the relationship and makes a commitment to do the right thing going forward. It also shows that parents aren't perfect but shows a commitment to do the best you can.

Sometimes young children don't see the need for an apology for something that they didn't mean to do. Examples would be spilling food or breaking a toy. Coach your child to make an apology something like this: "I'm sorry I spilled the juice. It was an accident. I'll clean it up." Again, modelling what to do in this situation is the way to help your children learn this. Be sure to apologize to your children and other family members if you bump into them or for accidental or unintentional mistakes.

Learning to make a sincere apology is a social skill and will improve with practice and maturity. Having your kids say the words, "I'm sorry," is just one part of the process.

27
WHAT'S WRONG WITH PRAISE?

Parents are advised to be supportive and encouraging with their kids, and that includes praising them. Praise is a good thing and every child needs to know that the people who love them think they are great. But is it possible to praise your kids too much? Much of this depends on the child's age.

Research has shown that frequent praise and encouragement is very effective with younger children, up to age three or four. It encourages effort and determination if it is linked to the child's efforts. Saying to a toddler who has been just learning this skill, "You put on your boots by yourself. Good for you!" is appropriate and encouraging. But saying the same thing to an eight-year-old would not be appropriate. If the child is going outside in winter, he must put on his boots and it's not something that warrants enthusiastic praise. As children get older, they respond differently to praise. They may find it manipulative, or if they are praised for something that they can do easily, they may start to question their own abilities.

A comment such as "Good job!" is often said by parents. We think the more that we praise a child, the more often we will see the behaviors we want. But with older children, sometimes what happens is that the praise is so frequent and easily earned that it loses its meaning and value. Such a short statement also doesn't make it clear what was "good" about it.

I remember praising my ten-year-old for a piece of homework he'd completed, and hearing his reply, "You're just saying that because you're my mom." He was right. It wasn't that great a piece of work, and my enthusiastic praise was my attempt to be positive and encouraging, to build his self-esteem. But my comment wasn't sincere or accurate and he recognized that.

I'm not saying don't praise your kids, but just don't overuse it. Many psychologists and parent educators believe that building self-esteem does not happen through praising everything your child does. Because it is so easily given, the praise becomes meaningless. Some kids become 'approval junkies,' always needing parent approval or praise for every little thing they do. So, be selective when and how you praise, and don't always use terms like 'fantastic!' if it's not. Some over-praised children get hooked on praise and may think they should get praised for everything, questioning whether they did okay if approval isn't clearly stated by their parents. Don't overstate your praise. A child shouldn't be praised to the sky simply for doing what is expected of everyone, such as showing up for a sports practice. Doing so is patronizing and can create self-doubt in children, rather than building their confidence and self-esteem.

Parenting experts suggest making the praise descriptive. For example, you might say, "I think your bed looks really good with how you smoothed out all the lumps and wrinkles in your covers." or, "That purple mountain in your drawing looks really nice." Descriptive praise shows that you have really paid attention to the child's efforts and aren't just using a common phrase like "fantastic" or "good job".

Avoid phrases like, "you were the best", "you're the smartest," or other comparative statements. Most children are smart enough to know what is true and realistic, and what is exaggeration. Too much unconditional praise seems like flattery and empty flattery at that. Children have a very clear idea of who really *is* the best at math or sports, and your inaccurate overstatements are more likely to make them feel that they have little worth if they are not the "best". Instead, focus on their efforts and not on comparing them to other children.

It is particularly important to praise your kids for their efforts, not for things that they have no control over. For example, praising a child's intelligence or good looks focuses on factors that are innate, not something that has anything to do with their own efforts. Instead, focus on the process of their activity: how hard they studied; that they carefully rewrote an essay; that they practiced their musical instrument for an extra 30 minutes. These are things that the child has control over and has to put in effort to achieve.

28
WHY DO TODDLERS HAVE SUCH CHALLENGING BEHAVIORS?

It's a bit of a shock when your cooperative baby starts to express his own wishes, often very loudly! For many toddlers, the words 'No' and 'Mine' are some of the first clear ones. And usually the words are said loudly and very definitely. Toddlers may have sudden bouts of crying, or tantrums; they may bite or hit. What parents might think of as an 'attitude' or being stubborn is not that at all. Parents shouldn't worry that a determined and strong-minded toddler will become a defiant teenager. These behaviors are a normal part of development and are an important developmental milestone. Toddlers are developing a sense of self—learning that they are separate people from their parents and that they can have an impact on their world. Toddlers are trying to communicate to get what they want and need.

For example, a toddler wants a toy that is too high to reach and shouts, yells and points until an adult gets it for her. If you are not sure what she is communicating and fail to respond, the toddler may scream and cry. Or, if the item is something unsafe that she should not have, and you refuse, the toddler will yell and get angry that her wishes are not being met. Toddlers are not developmentally ready to share and are very possessive of anything they are playing with. Most toddlers are very interested in other children, but they will only engage in parallel play, which is playing near each other. Additionally, they are not able to understand danger and can't understand why they can't touch, eat or play with any item that interests them, including such adult things as hot beverages or sharp items. It's up to parents and caregivers to help toddlers make sense of their world and to guide them to appropriate social and emotional skills. With toddlers, patience, consistency and distractions are good ways to deal with their misbehavior. They will slowly learn what is acceptable and what is not, if a parent uses a positive parenting style. While playing with your toddler, you can model taking turns and sharing. Be consistent about off-limits items or behavior (such as standing on a table, pulling the dog's fur, etc.) Parents can also ignore some behaviors, to avoid reinforcing the activity. For example, if your toddler throws his spoon on the floor over and over, he is experimenting with cause and effect. If you immediately jump up and pick up the spoon for him, that behavior can become a game. You'll get tired of that game a lot sooner than your toddler will!

Order and routines are very important for all children, and particularly for toddlers. When your toddler knows what will happen next in the day, it's much easier for him to make transitions from one activity to another and to cooperate. He should also have a safe play space that he can explore without a lot of restrictions.

Still, even with the best parenting possible, toddlerhood is a very tiring and challenging stage of parenthood. Try to enjoy all the learning and development that happens so quickly during this age, and know that with time, maturity and your positive guidance, things will get easier.

29
TEMPER TANTRUMS

One of the most common concerns that parents have is about temper tantrums. Numerous parenting books and parent education courses discuss the issue, because it's a common question from parents. It's very upsetting as a parent to see your child yelling, screaming, kicking and being out of control. Our own emotions get ramped up as we try to deal with this situation. And if we show anger, that tends to make the situation worse. Children have different temperaments and some are more easily angered and frustrated than others. Parents can try to prevent meltdowns or at least decrease the frequency and intensity of tantrums but be prepared—this is normal behavior in children between the ages of 18 months and four years. The peak frequency is between 18 months and three years. Even the most easy-going child may have a tantrum, especially when they are facing stress, new situations, noisy or overwhelming settings, or are tired or hungry.

Regardless of these factors, there is one reason for tantrums. They happen when a child doesn't get what he wants. You might not allow your child to do something that you think is unsafe, or have another cookie, or stay up too late, or refuse his bath. There can be any reason at all, sometimes something so minor that we adults are in disbelief. Your child might have a meltdown over the color of shirt you are trying to put on her or that you parked the train engine in the wrong spot while playing.

There are two general kinds of tantrum responses that I've observed when a child is opposing what you have decided. The first is when the child is in complete meltdown and has no control over her actions. With younger toddlers, their limited speech ability can cause them to react in a tantrum, when their parent doesn't respond with what they want after a few attempts at communicating. As communication skills improve, tantrums usually become less frequent. Try to figure out what your young child wants, *before* he gets frustrated and has a tantrum. Offer items or point to things, asking, "Is this what you want?" or "Show me what you want". Some parents teach simple signs so that babies and toddlers can communicate their wants before speech has developed. But if your child is in a full-out tantrum or meltdown, her emotions have taken over. She can't reason when she is in this state. The reasoning part of the child's brain is simply not working. So, don't try to reason with your child, or explain, bribe or threaten. Your child really can't comprehend what you are saying at this time. Explaining will do no good. (You can reason and explain after your child becomes calmer).

When a child is in a full-out emotional tantrum, you should make sure that the area is safe. If your child is likely to fling herself onto the floor, quickly move any items that could hurt her. Move slightly away so that you will not get hit or kicked. Stay calm and wait for the tantrum to subside. Don't try to reason with her but be nearby.

Your child needs to know that you are there and are someone they can count on. Some children will respond well to a big firm hug. Others can be distracted. For example, you could just start reading a book, or start a task such as stacking blocks or organizing toys. Do anything that might catch the interest or attention of your child. Sometimes picking up your child and taking her to another part of the house can help. Keep your voice soft and calm.

The second type of tantrum that I've observed is much more intentional. In this type, your child is yelling, crying, and angry, but seems to still have some control of his actions. The child is using this type of behavior to get what he wants and does have some control over his emotions. This happens when parents, with the best of intentions, have previously done things that actually increase the frequency of tantrums. To avoid reinforcing tantrum behaviors, here are a couple of key points to remember:

For many children, *any* attention, even negative attention, is better than no attention at all. Don't yell, or pay too much attention to the tantrum, (unless it seems that the child might hurt himself or others). Pay lots of attention to your child when he is behaving appropriately and cooperatively. Try to ignore any behavior that you don't want to see more of. Above all, DO NOT GIVE IN. This is simply teaching your child that a tantrum works to get what he wants. Here's an example. A toddler is allowed to eat one cookie and wants another. The parent feels that one cookie is enough and says, "No, only one cookie before supper." The toddler then starts to scream, point and yell, wanting another cookie. He might try to climb up on something to reach the cookies. After a few minutes of high volume, the parent can't take anymore, thinks, "oh well, it's only one more cookie," and gives in. The toddler stops screaming and enjoys the cookie. The parent has just reinforced the tantrum behavior, and you can bet the toddler's tantrums will become more frequent, because it worked. It's particularly a problem when a parent holds off and does not give in to the tantrum for a long time, but then finally does give in just to have some peace. Now the parent has taught the child not to give up, but to keep yelling and screaming for as long as it takes to get that cookie. If you are at home, ignore the tantrum if there is no danger. Don't ignore if the child does something that is related to the reason for the tantrum. In the cookie situation above, if your child moves a chair over to the counter to climb up and take the cookie that they want, then you must intervene and stop them.

Tantrums in a public place can make a parent feel embarrassed and guilty. You may feel you are being judged by others on your parenting or feel badly that others are disturbed by your child's behavior. Know the signs of potential trouble brewing, and leave the location with your child before the full-out tantrum starts. Just quietly leave and remind yourself that every parent has gone through this. If you meet someone's eyes, you might be pleasantly surprised to see a smile and a look of empathy, rather than that judgmental look you expected. Give your child a few minutes to calm down or carry him out of the area. Later, talk calmly and reasonably about what happened, your child's feelings, what you expect from him. Remind him that you will not give in.

Sometimes you may need to take your own "time out", doing some deep breathing and stretching to calm yourself down. If your home is safe and childproofed, you can remove yourself from the immediate area of your child for a few moments. Remember, if you don't reinforce the tantrums, they will diminish over time.

30
ENCOURAGING INDEPENDENCE

Most parents have felt frustrated by their preschool child saying, (often in a whiny voice), "I can't do it!" when we know she is perfectly able to do the task of putting a toy away, placing her shoes by the door, or hanging a jacket on a hook—all reasonable requests of a three or four-year-old. Then, you'll see the same child at preschool easily and cooperatively doing all those things.

One of the keys to encouraging independence is expectation. If a child is capable of the task, and you expect this, then it will be much more likely to occur. The independence that parents observe at preschool is because of clear expectations, and also because the entire group is doing the same things. Children copy others, as all parents know, and they copy their peers in the group.

An example of independence that always makes me smile can be seen at an airport. Families travelling with small children can be seen walking long distances in an airport, each pulling a rolling suitcase, including small children who look as young as three years old. What are the reasons for this ability to walk so far, being responsible for their suitcase, and showing so much independence? There are a few reasons. Everyone in the family is pulling or carrying a bag, and so are most others in the airport. Children observe that this is what people do and that this is the expectation. They observe what adults are doing, and try to copy their behavior, feeling a proud sense of independence. They also have a sense of ownership. Typically, they have a bag that is clearly theirs, with a superhero or movie character or bright color that they like. It's likely they have packed favorite toys, clothes or books, and they are taking responsibility for their special belongings. A smart parent has allowed them some choices about what to pack and has explained what to expect at the airport and what they will have to do.

To encourage independence at home, ask your child to help you with meaningful tasks that they have seen adults do, such as watering plants, pulling up weeds, setting the table, helping shovel snow, or baking. With personal hygiene tasks, allow them to do as much as they can on their own, brushing their hair, putting toothpaste on a toothbrush, washing hands and so on.

To develop a sense of ownership and responsibility, copy the ideas of early childhood teachers. Designate a certain shelf and hook for your child's shoes and jacket. Have a bookshelf or bin just for your child's books to encourage her to use them (and put them away) independently.

Another way to encourage independence and responsibility is to allow your child to have a certain regular household chore that is known to be their job and can be done independently. This should be a task that really needs to be done, not an invented type of chore. Some examples are: checking that the pet has water and refilling as necessary; putting cans and plastic bottles in the recycle bin; taking all the dirty laundry to the washing machine.

The tasks and expectations need to be age-appropriate for your child. If your child can put on his own jacket and boots, then let him do so, even if you are rushed or feeling a bit impatient. If you take over, redo their attempts to help with tasks, and do things that they can do for themselves, you will be sabotaging your goals of independence.

31
SHOULD KIDS DO CHORES?

The word 'chores' makes me think of farm chores; feeding the chickens, gathering eggs, grooming the horses and so on. Farm kids do chores as part of the family's work. Everyone does their chores, with responsibility based on age and ability… and everyone in the family benefits.

Nowadays with most people living in urban areas, farm chores are not familiar to most of us and are not required. But in every family, there is work to be done to keep a home clean, safe and healthy. We might not use the word 'chores', but that is what housework, cooking and yard work are.

Should parents expect and require their kids to help with these tasks? Some parents do and some do not. I remember a seventh-grade student complaining bitterly about her mom making her help with housework. I wondered if this young girl was being treated unfairly or harshly and asked her what she was required to do. "I had to clean my room and then she made me vacuum the

HALL," she answered indignantly. I didn't feel a lot of sympathy for her complaint. I believe strongly that as preparation for adult life, parents need to teach their kids about work and responsibility. If we want our kids to be independent we need to guide them to learn and practice the tasks that adults do, before they move out on their own. Of course, chores need to be age-appropriate and assigned fairly. Expecting a 12-year-old to vacuum is certainly within her ability and a fair request. She uses the whole house, not just her room, so being asked to clean other areas of the home is reasonable.

As well as being within a child's physical abilities, the chore should be within a child's emotional abilities. For example, you can expect a two-year-old to put away some toys in a basket, but likely you will need to help, encourage, model and maybe make a game of the task. A five-year-old can do the task alone, but if the toy-strewn room requires many minutes of work, the child might not have the patience to stick with it. You could say, "You put the blocks away and I'll put the books away." Breaking the large job into more manageable parts will help gain cooperation. You shouldn't expect a child to take on adult-type jobs, which are beyond their level of understanding and maturity. Be very clear in your instructions. "Please clean up your room," probably means something different to you than it does to your child. So be very specific. "Please make your bed. Put your dirty clothes in the hamper. Pick up all the toys and put them in the toy box."

Fairness is a big issue for kids. Try to be as fair as possible with siblings when assigning chores, remembering to adjust expectations for age and ability. Make sure that you are not allowing a less cooperative or procrastinating child to avoid helping while the more cooperative one ends up doing much more work. Avoid assigning certain jobs to boys and certain jobs to girls. *Everyone* needs to know how to cook, clean, cut the lawn, load a dishwasher, make a bed, do laundry and take out the garbage. Give your children some choice in the tasks they must do. For example, one child might prefer any type of job that takes them outside, while another might prefer to do things inside, or near the parent.

Everyone needs to help: parents, teenagers and young kids. Not only is this fair, it shows your kids that the family is a team, and that each family member is helping to keep the home running smoothly, so that everyone can enjoy it. When your kids grow up and live in a dorm room, apartment, house (or farm) the lessons they have learned from doing chores will be a huge help.

32
KIDS AND PHONES

There's a lot to discuss about your kid's phone use. How old should they be when they get a cell phone? Who pays for the phone and the monthly bill? What are the family rules around phone use?

First, you need to consider the existing expectations and routines in your home. Do you expect family meal time to be a time for conversation and for family members to be together? Are you trying to teach your kids financial responsibility? Are you careful about amount of sleep and bedtime routines with your kids? Do you think screen time should be limited to a certain amount of time each day? Once you are clear about those questions, you can set some rules around phone use, so that your child's cell phone doesn't have a negative impact on the existing routines in your home. Here are some suggestions from parenting education programs and parenting books for some basic rules for children and phones:

No phones at the dinner table, restaurants or during family games or movies.

No phones in the bedroom at bed time. Numerous studies have shown that having a phone in the bedroom interferes with sleep and mental health. Take the phone away at night and give it back in the morning. Some studies have shown that children and young teenagers actually are happy that they have an out from always being available on their phones. Some parents say the phone goes off at eight on school nights and ten pm on weekends.

Know the password. This is not an invasion of privacy. There have been too many cases of cyberbullying and worse.

If your child breaks or loses the phone, she will be responsible for cost of replacement.

If you wouldn't phone someone because it's too late at night or early in the morning, don't message them either.

Set up a charging station in an open area of the home such as the kitchen, and at night, so that all kids' cell phones are there, charging.

Make sure you know the school rules and support these rules. Some schools don't allow phones at all, some use them as mini-computers to support research in the classrooms, others allow them only during lunch breaks and after classes.

There are some great teen cell phone contracts on line, with all the rules and responsibilities that the family agrees on. You might want to ask your teen to add their own ideas.

Some common items included in these contracts are:

- Kids track their own usage and make sure they know how it impacts the monthly bill. Kids are responsible for any additional costs.
- No posting of any pictures without permission.
- No texting or messaging anything that you wouldn't say to a person's face.

- Nothing posted online that you wouldn't send or show to your parents or grandparents.

Remember, successful parenting is always about modelling. You can't expect your child to follow these expectations if you are not doing the same thing yourself. If you are constantly on your own phone, texting or checking social media, you can't expect your child to be any different.

33
KIDS AND ALLOWANCES

Most of us got an allowance when we were children. I can remember comparing what I got with what friends received and some of them got a lot more than I did! (I have to admit that some kids got less, and some didn't get an allowance at all.) Each week, my father gave us kids some cash. If we ran out of spending money, we had to wait for the next week. It seemed pretty straightforward, but from a parent's perspective, figuring out allowances for kids is a bit more complicated than it seems at first. Here are some things to think about...

- Do you want to give your child an allowance? Why not just give him money when he asks for it?
- How old should children be when they start getting an allowance?
- How much should they get? (What's the going rate?)
- How often do you pay it?

- Does your child have to work, by doing household chores, to receive the allowance?
- What is the allowance intended for? Is it for low-cost items of choice, like entertainment, movies, candy, or is it to cover such things as clothes, shoes, transportation?

Parenting experts agree that an allowance is a key to helping your child understand money and expenses. It's a building block for financial literacy, which refers to the skills and knowledge that allow a person to make informed decisions about money and other financial resources. One of the reasons for giving a set amount of allowance, rather than just providing money when asked, is to create a situation like that in the real world of receiving a pay-cheque on a regular basis. Whether you are wealthy or not, kids need to know that money is not in endless supply, available to them whenever they ask.

You can start giving an allowance to children as young as age six or seven, but it depends on the child. Have a detailed conversation about the process or hold a family meeting, explaining how it works, what happens if they run out of money, what it can be spent on, what you will continue to pay for, and how often you will renegotiate the amount. You also will want to require your child to save a portion as part of their financial education. You may want to ask that some of it be earmarked for charity.

How much allowance you pay depends on your own situation, the age of the child, and what the allowance is for. If it's for candy and games, maybe three to four dollars a week are sufficient. If you expect your child to use his allowance for lunch money or bus money, of course it needs to be more. Some parents give 50 cents a week per year of age of the child (an eight- year-old would get $4.00 a week). Remember you are trying to help your child to learn to manage money as if it is the real world, so the allowance should not be large enough to buy everything she wants. Doing without, or not buying exactly what you want, is part of adult life.

In my view, parents should pay for necessary things such as bus fare and lunches, and the allowance is for more discretionary items. That way, if a child runs out of money or spends foolishly the consequences are not too terrible. Older children age 10 and up may be able to handle their own lunch money and 12 and up may be able to have an allowance that covers the cost of clothes.

Many parents find it easiest to pay the allowance on the same day once a week. Once a month would be quite a large sum, and younger children might find it very hard to make the money last, leading to requests for more money, or disappointments. As children mature you might want to change the weekly schedule to twice a month or monthly to give them practice in budgeting.

Most parenting experts don't recommend linking the allowance to household chores. The idea is that as a family, everyone does their part, without having to be paid. Otherwise you might have a child refusing to take out the garbage, walk the dog, or tidy his room if he still has money left over from the week before. But you *can* offer the opportunity to earn more money to your child, if they are willing to do a task that you would not normally expect, or that you would pay someone else to do. Examples might be cleaning out the garage or washing windows.

Providing an allowance to children is an excellent tool for teaching financial responsibility.

34
SHOPPING AND FINANCIAL LITERACY

Financial literacy refers to the skills and knowledge that allow a person to make informed decisions about money and other financial resources. Financial literacy for kids? That sounds kind of complex, and maybe over their heads. But your children will have money at their disposal from quite a young age. Allowances, birthday presents of cash, gifts of money or store cards from grandparents will start coming their way. Kids as young as three can understand buying, spending and saving. We don't want our kids to reach adulthood and suddenly be thrown into the real world of budgeting. We all can tell stories about many young adults (and older adults) who struggle with financial decisions and are unable to manage their income and expenses. Money worries are one of the biggest causes of family breakdown. And a lot of the money worries come from spending beyond income. We need to start teaching our kids financial management skills from a very early age. Smart shopping is one of the keys to financial management and it's an activity you can show your kids very early.

When shopping for clothes, it can be easy to overspend. Kids might not understand the difference between needs and wants. Rather than buy something for each child to treat each child the same, take the opportunity to teach the difference between needs and wants. For example, one of your kids may need new shoes because the old ones are too small, but another sibling's shoes are still in good shape and fit well. You can explain that the shoes are *needed*, and that maybe soon the other child will get something new and her sibling won't. Go through the closets and shoe shelf together to see what is really needed. Keep items clean and in good repair; be sure to model taking care of shoes and clothing.

Try to shop in the off season. For example, summer clothing is often on sale by June, before the weather has even gotten hot. You can show your kids the price tags and sale prices. Go to the sale racks first. Comparison shop. Kids need to know that the same item can have different prices at different stores. Online shopping can be inexpensive but be sure to show your kids the sometimes hidden costs, such as shipping.

Kids need to know that using a debit (or credit) card is spending. One parent tells a story of explaining to her young child that she didn't have enough money to buy a toy. The child's response was, "Use the bank card." This was certainly a teachable moment to help children understand that a debit or credit card is not an unending source of money.

If you think something is too expensive, such as a certain brand of jeans, have a set amount in mind that you had planned to spend on the new jeans. If that isn't enough to buy the brand she wants, she might want to use her own savings to make up the difference. This helps children identify how much they really value that purchase. Sometimes, what happens is the child decides she doesn't want those jeans so badly after all, not enough to warrant spending her OWN money on them. Or, she realizes that she could buy a less expensive brand and still have money left over for something else. You may need to explain that if you pay that much for jeans, there will be no money for other needed items.

This is a good life lesson. As adults, we must make purchasing decisions, do without some things, resist having to have the 'latest' thing, and delay many major purchases. Successful parenting includes teaching and modelling financial life skills. There are a lot of great parenting resources about financial literacy for kids online.

35
HELPING YOUR TEENS TO BE REALISTIC ABOUT MONEY

Only a small percentage of people are wealthy and almost every adult has to make choices about spending and saving that involve doing without some things we want. What we earn frames our choices around the homes we live in, the cars we drive, the vacations we take, the clothes we buy, our charitable donations...and on and on. Living within your means is an essential concept and one that parents need to help their children to understand. This can be one of the most difficult things for teenagers to realize, especially if you, as a parent, have tried to provide everything they want. At the heart of living within your means is an understanding of needs and wants.

At my teens' high school, many of the teenagers' cars were much newer and nicer than the teachers, purchased for them by their parents for various milestones or birthdays. Some of us parents began discussing this, wondering how many teens have more money to spend on themselves at age 16 than they would ever have again. Would their adult earnings provide the kind of car, vacations, travel, clothes, and home that they had been used to? Would they be dissatisfied as young adults when they realized they couldn't have the same lifestyle that their parents had provided? Or, would they be motivated to study, work hard and try to achieve financial independence? We didn't come to an agreement in our discussion, but one thing we did agree on, was that advertising has created a situation in which many people have trouble telling the difference between needs and wants.

It's important for children and teens to understand the difference. It can be tricky but basically, such things as food, shelter, clothing, transportation and communication are 'needs', while 'wants' are those things we can do without. For example, the need may be for food, but the want is to go out to a restaurant. Parents can help their children understand the difference through discussion. For example, you need transportation, but it doesn't have to be a car of your own. Having a vehicle for our family is a need, but having a certain size or model is a want.

You can go look through the closet to identify which of the items are wants and which are needs. When it's time for back to school shopping, go through last year's supplies and see what can be reused, or what is worn out or too small. When it's time for clothes shopping, shoes that fit are a need, but a designer bag is a want. One teenager, after getting his first part-time job, described how he figured out the difference between needs and wants. His needs were still being taken care of by his parents (food, shelter, transportation, clothing, school supplies and fees). So, for wants, he looked at how many hours of work it took to earn the cash for the item and asked himself if that item was worth the four hours of his time and hard work. Sometimes his answer was yes, but often it turned out to be no, and he decided against the purchase, or bought a less expensive but similar item.

For teens, you can show them the utility bills, phone bill and grocery bills, talk about the real costs of having a home, renting an apartment and owning a car. (Many teens think the price of a car is all they must consider, so show them the costs of registration, insurance, repairs, tires and how much fuel costs.) Teens also need to learn about taxes and should have an idea of what taxes adults are required to pay. When they are thinking about getting a job, they need to know about the difference between gross and net income, and the taxes and employment deductions that will come off their pay-cheque. They also will need your help to make sure they file their tax return in the spring.

They should have an idea of what the average pay is for types of work, and then they can see how far that goes in covering expenses. Many teens simply do not know what expenses are for a typical family. They are shocked by the cost of groceries and all the other expenses. As parents, we need to help our teens prepare for the adult world by helping them distinguish between needs and wants and providing facts about income and expenses.

36
SHOULD YOUR TEEN HAVE A PART-TIME OR SUMMER JOB?

Most kids will have earned some money by babysitting, cutting the lawn, or doing some major task that you may pay them for. But a huge milestone in life is the first job. This usually happens at or after age 16 and is part-time.

Parents have differing views on whether their teenager should work outside the home either part-time or in a summer job. If the parents can provide for all their teen's needs and wants, parents may see no point to part-time work, concerned that studies or athletics will suffer. Others believe, and I would agree, that the lessons learned at a part-time job far outweigh any disadvantages. These benefits are much broader than just earning more spending money. So much is learned about the real world and the expectations that come with adulthood and a full-time career. For the first time, a teen will experience being under the authority and supervision of an adult other than their parent or teacher. They learn about rules that apply to every employee, and they are treated as an adult, just like any other employee. They get paid for what they do, they learn new skills, and they interact with people of diverse ages and backgrounds. They learn to get along with others and about different behavior expectations. In a customer service job, they learn to be polite to everyone, even difficult people, modifying their reactions and language. They must follow instructions, complete tasks within a time frame set by others, and do some unpleasant tasks that they might not want to do. It can be quite an eye opener for teens to see the tasks that many adults do to earn a living.

They feel like an adult and feel proud of their accomplishments. The part-time wage seems like a lot of money to most teens. Earning a regular wage encourages short and long-term goal planning. Some teens save toward a special trip, a car, or sports equipment, while others are working to help the family if family income needs a boost. Teens have a real sense of pride when they earn money independently.

Things might not always go smoothly in the workplace for your teen. Some kids get reprimanded, even fired—which may not be such a bad thing if it was a natural consequence of their own behavior in not meeting the expectations of the employer. Some teens who don't want to follow a dress code, find it difficult to be on time, don't show up when they have a leisure activity or event they don't want to miss, may end up being fired. I remember one teen I know who was fired for often being late for a morning shift at an electronics store. He was friendly, polite and knowledgeable, but none of that made a difference to the reality of the employer needing to rely on him to be there to do the job. It's a good life lesson when a teen learns that a work schedule means that you will not be able to stay up late before a work day or attend every leisure activity you want to. It's another great lesson if a teen realizes that having a supervisor or manager means they must follow their direction, even if they disagree. Teens learn that their value to the company or employer is based on their productivity, attitude and ability to do the job and that they can be replaced and will be, if they don't perform to a certain standard.

Another benefit of a teen job is exploring areas of work with an eye to the future. Your teen may realize that he has an interest in a certain employment sector or, on the other hand, may realize that he doesn't want to do that kind of work all his life. He can then think about his career goals and what training or education will be needed to work in the career he wants as an adult. So even if your family doesn't need the extra income, if you believe that your role includes helping your children to be ready for adult responsibilities, then a part-time job is one of the most helpful experiences of all.

37
HELPING YOUNG CHILDREN WHEN NATURAL DISASTERS STRIKE

When a terrible event such as a tornado, wildfire, flood or other natural disaster happens, it's extremely traumatic for everyone affected. For children, such events can be especially difficult to cope with. Even after the event is over and they are physically safe, children may have difficulties, (although each child is different and there is no one typical way of responding). Children may be more irritable, less cooperative, have tantrums or regress from milestones such as being potty-trained or sleeping alone. There might be bed wetting or they might become very demanding and seem angry all the time. They might cling to you and be unable to let you out of their sight. Frequent crying, inability to sleep, and general loss of interest in activities or play can also occur.

What can parents do to help children through these times? Although it is difficult, parents need to keep calm themselves. One dad was asked how he could be smiling and playing with his kids after being evacuated from their home, not knowing if it was still standing, and his response was that he could act 'normal', because it was for his kids. That wise dad knew that his children needed to see their dad interacting, talking, laughing and smiling as he always had. His kids needed the comfort of that consistent adult, sending a message that everything was going to be okay. It might be acting, or 'putting on a front', but parents need to appear calm, confident and in charge. Save your times of adult conversation and worries for when your children are not around. Keep adult concerns for adult conversation. For example, a young child cannot handle the stress and anxiety of money concerns around food, shelter, clothing and your job. It's hard enough to deal with that as an adult.

Protect kids from too much live news, updates, and dramatic video. Seeing scenes of the event over and over increases stress as the child relives the experiences. Although they want to know what's going on, you need to filter the information. Follow their lead about what they want to talk about, by asking what they have been hearing and giving them answers to their questions, but in a simple way. Don't volunteer more information than they ask about; remember they are children and you need to keep things appropriate to their level of development and understanding. You don't want them to imagine things to be worse than they really are. You can expect to have these conversations frequently with some children; as they try to come to terms with the situation, they may talk often about it and ask the same questions over and over.

To help everyone cope, be sure to eat regular, nutritious family meals, be physically active and try to get enough sleep. Set some sort of daily routine, even if you are no longer going to work or are living away from your home.

Children can act out their feelings about the events through play. They may want to write a letter or a story, or younger children can dictate a story to you. Drawing pictures can be a good way for children to express their feelings. Find times to have fun and play with your kids and encourage time with friends. Children may be feeling helpless and powerless. Involve them in ways that they can help with the situation.

A story from Fred Rogers, of *Mr. Rogers' Neighborhood*, may help everyone with their feelings of distress and fear: "When I was a boy, and I would see scary things in the news, my mother would say to me, 'Look for the helpers. You will always find people who are helping.'"

38
LAST THOUGHTS

Here are some key points about wise parenting:
- To encourage speech development and reading and later success in school, make sure you read to your children every day, starting when they are babies. Make a simple goal of reading for 10 minutes a day. Talk frequently with your children, right from birth. Explain things, ask questions, point out things you observe and use new words to help them expand their vocabulary.
- Your child will have lots of friends and classmates throughout his life, but he will only have one or two parents. Your role as a parent is important and unique. Your child needs a caregiver, protector and guide, not another pal.

- You are a role model for your children, whether you intend to be or not. Children are always watching and listening and will copy your actions, good or bad. Be sure they are seeing and hearing the things you want them to.
- If you feel overwhelmed by trying to do everything 'right' for your kids, focus on small changes that you can easily make. Maybe try something as simple as having a family meal together each day or limiting screen time.

For most of us, being a parent is the most important job we will ever do. Have fun doing it, while taking on this huge responsibility.

ABOUT THE AUTHOR

Laurie Lafortune has worked for over 30 years in the human services and education fields. She began her career as a middle-years teacher and then focused on early childhood education, working as a preschool teacher, parenting instructor, consultant, college instructor and director for early years organizations. Most recently, Laurie was a team member on two major early childhood development research projects in Canada. Laurie has provided numerous workshops and training events for parents and caregivers. A mother of three and a grandparent, Laurie cares deeply about the well-being of children and believes that every child deserves a great start in life, with the loving guidance of family.

www.ingramcontent.com/pod-product-compliance
Lightning Source LLC
Chambersburg PA
CBHW071517040426
42444CB00008B/1694